the Healthy College Cookbook

Quick. Cheap. Easy.

Alexandra Nimetz · Jason Stanley · Emeline Starr

 Storey Publishing

The mission of Storey Publishing is to serve our customers by publishing practical information that encourages personal independence in harmony with the environment.

Edited by Nancy Ringer and Gwen Steege
Photography © Jeff Burke and Lorraine Triolo for Artville
Cover & text design and production by Mark Tomasi
Indexed by Nan Badgett, Word•a•bil•i•ty

Storey books are available for special premium and promotional uses and for customized editions. For further information, please call 1-800-793-9396.

Printed in the Canada by Transcontinental
25 24 23 22 21 20 19 18 17 16

Library of Congress Cataloging-in-Publication Data

Nimetz, Alexandra, 1977–
    The healthy college cookbook : quick, cheap, easy / Alexandra Nimetz, Jason Stanley, Emeline Starr.
        p.   cm.
    ISBN-13: 978-1-58017-126-7 (pbk. : alk. paper); ISBN-10: 1-58017-126-5 (pbk. : alk. paper)
    1. Cookery.   2. Quick and easy cookery.   I. Stanley, Jason, 1977– .   II. Starr, Emeline, 1975– .
    III. Title.
TX715.N683   1999
641.5'55—dc21   98-55398
                                                                                          CIP

Dedication

To our families

Contents

Acknowledgments

While our three names appear on the cover of this book as its authors, there are many more people who contributed behind the scenes to its ultimate publication. To those who contributed recipes, those who taste-tested our experiments, and those who offered support in other ways, we appreciate your helpfulness along the way. In particular, thank you to Amy Aloysi; Natalie Andre; Neal Appleman; Danielle Bahr; Allison Bergman; Meghan and Heather Brady; Alex Bresnan; Beth, Brendan, and Mary Buschman-Kelly, and Mary Kelly; Alison Cantatore; Tong Chen; Kip Darcy; Laura Davis; Maya Dehart; Rachel Dubin; Rachel Felsenthal; Katie Fogg; Mary Frekko; Lolly Gaul; Satie Gopaul; Lauren Greilsheimer; Anna Groskin; Peter Hardin; Matthew Karagus; Kim Karetsky; Beth Lambert; Katherine Landry; Patti Lin; Brett Linck; Tangee Mahdui; Sabina Menschel; Matthew, Gloria, Lloyd, and Meaux Nimetz; Dede, James, and John Orraca-Tetteh; Jon Putman; Sharon Rackow; Derek Sasaki-Scanlon; Emily Shanks; Frank, Paula, Bryce, Scott, Matthew, and Benjamin Stanley; Dan, Judy, Nick, and Dan Starr; Meg Turner; Kelly Virgulto; Victoria Wallace; Katie Wallach; George Warner; Christina Witter; Wells P. Wilson; those at Creative Gardening; and those that we stopped along the road and in the supermarket to take our pictures.

Last, but certainly not least, thank you to Storey. Who would have thought that a brainstorming session in Pam's office during Winter Study '98 would have led to this?

Introduction

As we write this book, the three of us are all students at Williams College in Williamstown, Massachusetts. We don't have summer experience working as short-order cooks, nor have we ever attended a culinary school. Before beginning this project, we were like all of you: We often had no idea what to prepare for dinner and didn't have the time to whip up elaborate meals. This book was designed to answer our concerns (and yours) about how to eat healthfully on a tight budget, with a busy schedule, and with little cooking experience. Don't expect to see here lengthy lists of ingredients, confusing instructions, or long cooking times. In fact, many of the recipes in this book contain fewer than five ingredients. They are easy to cook and taste great. We know that it's easy to settle for unhealthy food when you don't have the time to prepare something, but we hope that this book will provide you with alternatives to the evils of fast food. You can make many of these recipes in the same time as it takes to have a pizza delivered. We know, because we've tested every recipe.

We believe the key to healthy eating is a balanced diet that includes a wide variety of foods. Those of you who have special dietary concerns — athletes, vegetarians, and those with family histories of high cholesterol, to name just a few — can examine the nutritional information to find the recipes best suited to your dietary regime. For those of you who are not as strict with your diet but still want to eat healthfully, you can rest assured that you'll find a great variety of simple, tasty recipes.

While we've tried to avoid using excessive amounts of oil and other fatty foods, please note that this is not a fat-free cookbook. It's not healthy to totally eliminate fat from your diet — plus, most food tastes pretty much like cardboard without it.

For those of you who are especially health conscious, we used computer software to formulate a brief nutritional analysis of the calorie, fat, protein, carbohydrate, cholesterol, and sodium content of each recipe. Because vegetarian options are becoming more in demand, we have also included a section solely devoted to them. However, as there are vegetarian recipes in other sections, we have marked all such dishes with a 🌿 so they'll be easy to recognize. In addition, our personal favorites — we voted, majority rules — are marked with a ★, and the especially quick recipes, those that take ten minutes or less to prepare, are marked with a ⏱ .

🌿 = Vegetarian

★ = Authors' Choice

⏱ = Super-Quick

In addition to providing recipes, the book opens with a few sections on getting started. For those of you who are moving into a new place with, perhaps, your first kitchen, there are a few pages on setting up — what kinds of cookware you'll need and a checklist for stocking the shelves with elementary ingredients. In case you'll be cooking from another cookbook (although we doubt you'll find one as useful as ours), using Mom's recipes, or experimenting on your own, we have also provided our own abridged dictionary of cooking terms and another of herbs and spices. There are tips on shopping for food, defrosting, reheating, and freezing, ideas for healthy substitutions, and other tidbits of information we have found helpful.

To all our users: We hope that after using this book you will have a more solid understanding of cooking in general and will no longer consider it to be a tedious or unrewarding task. We certainly have enjoyed writing and testing.

Good luck and enjoy.

ALEXANDRA NIMETZ
JASON STANLEY
EMELINE STARR

Chapter 1

Getting Started in Your First Kitchen

Cooking is like any other activity: In order to be successful and have fun in the process, you need to have the right equipment. We've thought long and hard about what really are the essentials for a novice cook's kitchen. The ideas and recommendations listed here will help you to develop a fully stocked and efficient kitchen, including the necessary hardware as well as useful foods to keep on hand.

In the following pages, you'll find a glossary of terms that may pop up throughout this book and other cooking guides, which may help you to understand the basics of cooking. You will also find descriptions of common herbs and spices and some of their most frequent companions. In addition, we'll hand down to you tips we've learned along the way, healthy substitutions for some not-so-healthy ingredients, and charts to help you with measurement and temperature conversions.

Our most important piece of advice? Take your time, relax, and don't be afraid to get creative!

Setting Up Your Kitchen

A bare kitchen can be an intimidating place for beginners, especially when it becomes obvious that you will have to equip your kitchen with some essentials. While it's not necessary to spend tons of money on top-of-the-line kitchenware, it is important to invest in the basics.

Shopping for your kitchen can be a tedious task, since exactly what it is that you need to buy is not always clear. Sure, a pot, a skillet, and a mixing spoon may come speeding to mind, but what about a measuring cup or an oven mitt? To facilitate your shopping expedition, we have provided a list of items that we feel, after making all of the recipes in this book, are necessities for any kitchen. You may decide, based on your eating habits, that you don't need to invest in all the items we suggest. If so, this will not offend us in any way — every cook's kitchen is different.

Cookware

If you're lucky, you're moving into a furnished house with a fully equipped and stocked kitchen. For those of you who are not so lucky, the key to building a comfortable and functional kitchen is to give up dreams of endless stainless-steel and Teflon-coated pots and pans. Instead, keep an eye out for the bargains. Buy cookware with multiple uses and organize your storage space (which, if your apartment is anything like the ones we've had, will be limited) so that the pots and pans you use most often are easy to grab.

In the interests of preserving your budget, keep in mind that you can usually pick up many of these items at yard sales or at a local second-hand store. This is especially true for the electrical equipment, such as microwaves, beaters, and blenders, which can be expensive in a department store but cost next to nothing at a tag sale.

Mom's Tips

If you have a small kitchen, purchase pots, pans, strainers, and spoons with loops or clasps for hanging. Install hooks (small nails will also do) in the kitchen walls and hang as much of your cookware as possible. It's an incredibly efficient use of space and keeps the cookware easily accessible yet out of the way when not in use.

Mixing bowls: You'll find that you need more than one, so buy at least one medium-size and one large bowl.

Skillet: Otherwise known as a frying pan. Look for a heavy, durable pan with a nonstick surface. You may want a couple of different sizes — we suggest a 7-inch and a 10-inch.

Pots: Again, you will want a couple. Get one small or medium-size nonstick saucepan (2- to 3-quart) and a pot big enough for making large quantities of pasta or soups (6-quart).

Casserole dish: Make sure the dish is ceramic or ovenproof glass. We recommend having a good large one, such as 11 by 7 inches.

Loaf pan: We highly recommend having at least one loaf pan, as it is good not only for making breads but also for smaller casseroles.

Cookie sheet: Buy one with a nonstick surface. (If you're a cookie maker, you'll want at least two.)

Cutting boards: Buy two — one for cutting meat and one for everything else. Keep them scrupulously clean, as they can be a carrier for food-borne bacteria.

Measuring cups: Buy a full set or two large ones.

Measuring spoons: Buy a full set and keep them separate from the rest of your silverware.

Grater: Box graters are stronger than flat graters and less likely to collapse under pressure.

Strainer: Strainers with "feet" that you can set in the sink are easy to use and clean.

Spatula: Buy one with a sturdy head for flipping pancakes, removing cookies from cookie sheets, and other such tasks. If your spatula has a plastic head, be sure not to leave it on the stove — it will melt!

Can opener: You may starve if you don't have one of these.

Wooden or stainless-steel mixing spoons: You'll need these for mixing and stirring. Wooden spoons won't scratch the surface of your nonstick pots and pans.

Large knife: It's worth your money to buy a good, durable knife. Going cheap will cost you more in aggravation in the long run.

Paring knife: A smaller knife is much easier to use for small jobs.

Vegetable peeler: If you're going to be eating healthy, you'll be eating vegetables at some point, and this will come in handy.

Oven mitts: Buy two.

Dish towels: Buy at least three — one will always be dirty, one you can use to clean up as you cook, and the other should be left for drying dishes.

Garlic press: If you're a big fan of garlic, this tool will be invaluable. Invest in a good-quality press and you'll have fresh minced garlic whenever you want it, and you won't have smelly fingertips.

Plastic containers: These will be useful for saving leftovers. Instead of investing in high-priced Tupperware, however, just wash and save the empty containers that held yogurt, cottage cheese, peanut butter, and other foods.

Silverware, cups, bowls, and plates: You can usually pick these up cheap at yard sales or your local secondhand store.

Blender: It's good for purees, pestos, and margaritas alike.

Microwave: Although certainly not necessary, it does make the quick meal even quicker.

Stocking the Shelves

Now that you have equipped your kitchen, you'll want to stock up on some essential food items. As we've learned from experience, it's quite common to begin preparing a dish only to realize ten minutes later, mid-recipe and mid-mess, that a necessary ingredient is nowhere to be found. We hope to help you minimize the frustration and trauma that can result from these scenarios by providing a list of useful items to keep in your kitchen.

We've presented this information in a checklist form to make it easy for you while you're shopping. While you may think that you'll remember everything you need when at the supermarket, we guarantee that you won't. So don't hesitate to take this book with you. Just don't leave it in the cart!

CABINET ESSENTIALS

- ❏ Rice
- ❏ Pasta
- ❏ Tomato sauce
- ❏ Canned tomatoes
- ❏ Red wine and balsamic vinegar
- ❏ Extra-virgin olive oil and/or canola oil
- ❏ Nonstick cooking spray
- ❏ Bouillon cubes
- ❏ Bread
- ❏ Cereal

- ❏ Peanut butter
- ❏ Canned tuna fish
- ❏ Flour
- ❏ Sugar
- ❏ Salt and pepper
- ❏ Baking powder
- ❏ Baking soda
- ❏ Vanilla extract
- ❏ Soy sauce (low-sodium)
- ❏ Aluminum foil and plastic wrap

Filling the Fridge

The next space to fill is your refrigerator. Again, you will find that you probably want to start with some basics that are always useful to have on hand. Just remember, they have to be replaced more frequently than the canned goods in your cabinets.

Mom's Tips

Rice Tips

▸ To cook, use one cup plus a splash of water for every cup of rice. Cover, bring to a boil, reduce heat, and simmer until all the water is absorbed. Taste the rice. If it still isn't cooked, add a little more water and continue cooking.

▸ One cup of uncooked rice will yield about two cups of cooked rice.

▸ Add a few drops of water to rice (or any rice-based dish) when reheating in a microwave. This will keep it from becoming dry.

- ❑ Butter or margarine
- ❑ Cheese
- ❑ Milk
- ❑ Eggs
- ❑ Jam or jelly
- ❑ Ketchup
- ❑ Mayonnaise
- ❑ Mustard

Cooking Terms

Sometimes cooking terminology can be confusing. We have done our best throughout this book to keep terminology simple and to the point. Just in case, however, we've included a brief list of frequently used terms and their definitions so that there will be no misunderstandings. In addition to this basic vocabulary, we have included a few other commonly and not-so-commonly used terms that are useful for impressing friends and family.

Bake: To cook food in an oven with dry heat. Unless otherwise specified, always preheat your oven before putting your dish in to bake.

Barbecue: Although barbecuing technically refers to cooking over a charcoal grill, it has evolved to denote just about anything, including roasting, broiling, or grilling, that involves barbecue sauce.

Baste: The point of basting is to keep roasting foods, usually meat, moist by reapplying sauce, pan juices, wine, or whatever liquid you're using. You have all seen turkey basters, those giant eye droppers hidden somewhere in your parents' kitchen. They're used to suck up the liquid collecting in the bottom of the pan and dribble it back on top of the roast. Basting can also be accomplished by brushing or spooning the liquid onto the food.

Beat: Rapidly mixing ingredients. Should result in a smooth, airy mixture.

KITCHEN
QUICK TIP

Three Easy Odor-Beaters

1. Food storage containers made of plastic can absorb odors easily. To rid them of the smell, soak the containers in a solution of 1 tablespoon baking soda per cup of hot water.

2. To rid your microwave of bad odors, place a glass of water mixed with 2 tablespoons lemon juice inside and microwave on high for 2 minutes.

3. To absorb odors in your refrigerator, keep an opened box of baking soda tucked away somewhere. But don't use the same box for cooking; those odors will be transferred to your food. Change the box about every three months. And don't just throw the old box away when those three months are up; to freshen a sink, pour the baking soda down the drain and follow with hot water.

Blanch: The point of blanching is not to cook the food (usually a fruit or a vegetable), but rather to soften it so that it may be peeled more easily or cooked ever so slightly. Submerse the fruit or vegetable in boiling water for a minute or two (the length of time depends on the food). It should soften and the skin will become easy to remove. If you haven't blanched for long enough, the skin won't peel. If that's the case, just dip the food back in.

Blend: To mix well.

Breading: As the name suggests, to cover with bread. Dip the food in raw egg or milk, roll it in bread crumbs, place it in a dish, and bake. You can also bread with crushed corn flakes or potato chips, among other things.

Broil: To cook under or over a direct, intense heat. Broiling browns the outside of the food and seals the juices in. You can broil under the broiler in your oven or on a grill. (Some ovens require that the door be kept ajar when broiling.)

Boil: When you've heated a liquid to a boil, you'll see bubbles bursting up from the bottom of the pot. There are different degrees of boiling: a violent boil, a moderate (or rolling) boil, and a slow boil (simmer). Remember, a liquid is only boiling when bubbles are popping through the surface. It is not boiling when you see little bubbles resting on the bottom of the pot (although that means that you are close).

Burn: If you are having success with this one, you probably should not be left alone in the kitchen.

Chop: This dictionary definition, "to cut with an ax or sharp-edged tool; make chopping blows (at)," may not be the best suggestion for your purposes. The general idea is to cut into small pieces. If you're going to be cooking the food you're chopping, make sure that the pieces are all approximately the same size so that they'll cook evenly.

Cream: To cream does not mean to add cream to a mixture but rather to fully soften an ingredient, such as butter. When creaming, you will often have to blend in other ingredients, such as sugar, until the mixture is completely "creamed" or blended together.

Dice: To cut into very small cubes, usually about half an inch (1 cm) in length and width.

Fry: Though fried food tastes great, it's not usually considered the healthiest of cooking techniques. Break out the skillet and throw some oil or butter in. Heat the pan on the burner and then pop the food in. Be careful with hot oil. Not only can it hurt if you're splattered (boiling oil will spit at you when foods, especially liquids, are added) but it is also a big fire starter if left unattended. See also *Sauté*.

Grate: Technically speaking, to grate means to reduce to small particles — just think of grated Parmesan cheese. Using a grater will save you the trouble of painstakingly chopping and shredding foods into small pieces.

Gratin: *Au gratin* is a French term meaning "with cheese." You can make anything *au gratin* by sprinkling some grated cheese, butter, and bread crumbs over the top of a dish and then broiling it until golden. Looks good when finished and sounds fancy for dinner parties.

Marinate: This takes a little while to do, but don't worry — you won't be doing much of the work, the marinade will be. Marinade is the liquid (usually flavored with various spices) that you soak a food in. The marinade will flavor the food while at the same time tenderizing it (if you're marinating meat). This will make cheaper, tougher meat taste much better. And experiment with your creations. They won't all work well, but you'll come across some that you love.

Mince: To cut or chop into extremely, very, ultra-small pieces.

Poach: To cook by simmering in a liquid that does not quite reach a boil.

Preheat: To set the oven or broiler to the desired temperature 10–15 minutes before use to allow time for it to reach the appropriate temperature prior to cooking.

Puree: Remember baby food? Well, it's food, pureed, so it can be swallowed at that toothless age. Pureeing by hand is great for venting aggravation. Just smash and pound the food until it's a pulp. You may have to boil some vegetables to soften them first (unless you're really upset). Most people, however, understand puree to mean putting something in the blender or food processor, since it does the hard work for you. The blades turn and miraculously your solid food is transformed into a creamy consistency.

Sauté: To cook food in a buttered or oiled pan until slightly brown. Sautéing is similar to frying, but implies that you use less butter or oil and stir the dish constantly.

Reconstitute: To rehydrate a dry food by adding liquid.

Reduce: Reducing serves to concentrate flavor while at the same time cutting down on the total amount of liquid. You reduce something by boiling it for a while uncovered. This causes some of the liquid to evaporate, leaving a substance with less volume but more taste.

Shred: This slightly barbaric term refers to the act of tearing. You can use a knife or a grater to do so and, just like in a paper shredder, the pieces should come out relatively thin and long.

Simmer: To simmer is to keep something on low heat so that it does not quite reach a boil. You should hardly be able to notice any bubbles boiling up to the surface. The surface should just ripple a little.

Skim: To remove the top layer of something. For example, after refrigerating or freezing a broth, you'll notice a layer of hardened fat on the surface. Scoop it off and you've skimmed it. This is a good way to decrease the amount of fat in soups or gravies.

Tenderize: As you might guess, to make more tender. Some cooks like to gently pound cuts of meat, thus tenderizing them, before cooking or marinating.

Herbs and Spices

When we were first beginning to cook, our knowledge of cooking with herbs and spices was pretty much limited to salt, pepper, basil, and garlic and onion powder. We figure that most of you are probably in a similar boat. Although we wouldn't think of going into great depth here — there are entire volumes devoted to the subject at every bookstore — we hope to provide an overview of the basics.

We are not recommending that you buy all the herbs and spices mentioned in this section. That could be incredibly expensive. In order to preserve your budget yet still have meals with seasoning pizzazz, we suggest that you invest in a select few herbs and spices. Our personal favorites are basil, cinnamon, garlic, ginger, oregano, and peppercorns. We've found that they are called for in a lot of recipes and, with these six, you can find the right seasoning for just about any dish.

Dried herbs and spices come in small glass or plastic containers and can be found in your supermarket. Don't be afraid to buy no-name products. They usually cost considerably less and taste the same. If you have a natural foods store or cooperative in your area, you can also sometimes buy herbs relatively inexpensively from their bulk bins — simply weigh out an ounce or two to bring home, and save glass jars to store them in.

As for fresh herbs, there is no question that the real thing (as compared to the dried stuff) is far superior. However, when they're not in season, fresh herbs sometimes can be expensive or hard to find. So during the summer months, buy the more common herbs, such as thyme, basil, and cilantro, fresh from the produce aisle of the grocery store, but when the cold season hits, if prices go up, stick to dried herbs. If you have a sunny windowsill and the inclination, you might even try growing your own herbs. Many grocery stores with potted-plant departments carry herbs.

Herbs can be fun when you gain the confidence to experiment with them. Start with a little salt and pepper here and there, and then try adding new spices. Pretty soon you'll be whipping up sauces and dishes that you never dreamed you could create with your limited supplies. Just try to have fun with them and before you know it, you'll outgrow this beginner's overview.

Basil

This herb is an essential for your kitchen and your life. If you have the patience for occasionally watering a plant and you enjoy the taste of fresh basil, invest in a basil plant — you can find them at farmer's markets, garden shops, and even grocery stores. If you don't have a particularly green thumb but won't settle for the dried stuff you can usually buy bunches of basil in your supermarket, somewhere among the vegetables. It is great in anything tomato-related, such as pasta sauces and tomato-mozzarella-basil sandwiches, salads, pestos, and even with eggs.

Bay Leaf

If you ever wondered why there was a big, crispy leaf in your bowl of soup, you were obviously not familiar with the bay leaf. It's commonly used to enhance the flavors of soups, stews, and chilies — dishes that require a long simmering time — and should be removed from the dish before serving.

Cayenne

For instant hot, throw just a pinch of cayenne in the mix. Also known as ground or crushed red pepper, it's great for spicing up chilies, burritos,

Mom's Tips

Dried vs. Fresh

In most cases, fresh and dried herbs are interchangeable. If a recipe calls for fresh and you want to use dried, use half as much as the recipe calls for. If a recipe calls for dried herbs and you want to use fresh, use twice as much as the recipe calls for.

stir-fries, chicken, and even guacamole. However, be careful when adding cayenne powder to dishes. Remember, you can always add more.

Chili Powder

Chili powder is a mixture of ground dried chile peppers and other spices. The exact taste and strength of the powder depends on the brand you use. Try sprinkling some in sauces, on tomato dishes, on meat, and, of course, in chilies.

Chives

Chives belong to the onion family and, not surprisingly, have a taste somewhat similar to a young onion. They look like thick grass, and you can often see them growing wild. Fresh chives are so good that we suggest you consider buying a plant and keeping it in your kitchen — it's a very hardy plant, so even the most inattentive gardener can usually keep one alive. Chives are often called for in recipes for soups, salads, and eggs. If you like cottage cheese, try cutting up some chives and mixing them in. It's delicious. Really.

Cilantro

Even if you don't know what cilantro is, we suspect that you've probably tasted it, perhaps in a favorite salsa. Fresh cilantro looks similar to parsley and is one of those herbs that people either love or hate. We love it (at least two out of three of us do). When you can get it, the real thing is far superior to the dried herb. It has a strong taste that adds a fresh flavor to dips, soups, and, most commonly, salsa, including anything that salsa is used on, such as burritos or nachos.

Cinnamon

An extremely useful spice, cinnamon can be used in dessert dishes like apple pie or rice pudding, or in hot fruit drinks like hot cider. Sprinkle some on buttered toast with a little sugar and you have a fast and delicious snack.

Curry Powder

If you've ever had good Indian food, you'll appreciate curry powder. It is yellowish orange in color and, like chili powder, is a mixture of spices. Curry powder is good with rice, chicken, and vegetables.

Dill

While the dill plant looks rather delicate, it has a strong taste that is excellent in salads of any kind, including greens, plain cucumber, seafood, tuna, and potato salads. It is also delicious when used with carrots and fish (especially salmon).

Garlic

Garlic is great — in moderation that is. Although it is typically associated with relentlessly horrible breath, it's wonderful for spicing up an endless variety of dishes and boasts quite a few health benefits. If you don't like the smelly fingers that result from peeling and chopping cloves, consider buying a garlic press, or buy prechopped garlic, which comes in a jar and can be purchased at any grocery store. Although garlic lovers and herb purists may wince at this suggestion, yet another alternative is garlic powder. It's cheap, requires no preparation, and doesn't smell.

Ginger

As sushi lovers, some of us hold a special fondness for this spice. Ginger is a root and can be bought fresh in the produce aisle of your grocery store, in which case you'll have to grate or slice it. You can also buy ground dried ginger. We highly recommend that you buy one or the other, as ginger adds a terrific flavor to a wide variety of dishes. It makes a delicious addition to pureed vegetable soups and desserts, or can be mixed with some soy sauce as a marinade for meat, chicken, or salmon.

Mint

Although typically associated with sweet dishes like fresh fruit salad, a few sprigs of fresh mint (or a few pinches of it dried) are also delicious with peas and other vegetables. You can also use it in tomato sauces, especially those with meat, and it makes a wonderful hot or iced tea when steeped in water.

Onion

The sharp and pungent nature of onion is absorbed and mellowed when used in soups, pasta sauces, and meat dishes. Onion powder is a quick and easy alternative, but as onions have a relatively long shelf-life, we recommend stocking the real thing whenever possible and saving the powdered stuff for emergencies.

Oregano

Oregano is an essential ingredient of traditional Italian cooking. You can add it to just about any tomato-based dish and sprinkle it on most meats. It's pretty strong, so start with just a pinch and add more as needed.

Paprika

Paprika is a Hungarian spice that is made up of a variety of ground dried peppers. It is flavorful in hearty soups, sprinkled on top of meat or chicken, or mixed into spreads like hummus. As a bright red spice, it also serves to add great color to dishes — try sprinkling it on top of deviled eggs or tuna salad.

Parsley

If any taste is "green," it's parsley. In restaurants, you'll see parsley as a common garnish for dinner plates. Use it chopped as a condiment for baked potatoes, and use sprigs tossed with salads or for topping soups. Also important, parsley can help to deodorize your hands and breath after cutting or eating garlic. Parsley is usually available fresh year-round — don't bother buying the dried stuff.

Rosemary

Rosemary has a very pleasant smell and is sometimes used in incense. It keeps well as a dried herb, and is particularly tasty with tomatoes, potatoes, chicken, and lamb. Try a stir-fry with tomatoes, chicken, a little white wine, and rosemary served over rice — simple and quick with a touch of elegance.

Sage

If you can manage to use sage without getting Simon and Garfunkel tunes stuck in your head, you are doing better than we are. Dried sage is as good as the fresh plant and goes well with chicken, eggplant, and many soups and stews.

Thyme

Like rosemary, thyme is exceptionally aromatic. Try it in stews or hearty soups, vegetable mixes, and on meat or chicken. It's also pretty strong, so start with just a pinch and add more as necessary.

Complementary Herbs and Foods

The key to being creative in the kitchen is to teach yourself which herbs and spices create what flavors, and what they go well with. The following is a key to some of the most basic combinations. The mix-and-match ideas here will help you develop quick meals.

Seasonings for Vegetables

Asparagus	Lemon juice, dry mustard, or thyme
Broccoli	Lemon juice or dill
Brussels sprouts	Lemon juice; white-wine vinegar with dry mustard and/or dill
Cabbage	Lemon juice; white-wine vinegar with dry mustard and/or oregano
Carrots	Honey, maple syrup, thyme, or dill
Cauliflower	Parsley and nutmeg; dill and tarragon
Corn	Garlic; onion and paprika
Eggplant	Thyme, garlic, and oregano
Green beans	Garlic, onion, or dill

**Authors' Choice
Herbs and Spices**

These six herbs and spices are essential for every spice cupboard.

- Basil
- Cinnamon
- Garlic
- Ginger
- Oregano
- Freshly ground black pepper

Lima beans	Onions; sage; or lemon juice and parsley
Mushrooms	Garlic, onion, or basil
Peas	Rosemary or thyme (or both)
Potatoes	Onion or garlic (or both)
Sweet potatoes	Nutmeg or cinnamon
Tomatoes	Basil and garlic; chives
Winter squash	Brown sugar, maple syrup, nutmeg, or ginger

SEASONINGS FOR MEATS

In addition to salt and pepper, try some of the following:

Beef	Basil, garlic, oregano, onions, parsley, rosemary, thyme, allspice, cayenne, chili powder, cloves, or paprika
Eggs	Basil, chives, tarragon, or thyme
Fish	Basil, dill, chives, parsley, rosemary, thyme, or tarragon
Lamb	Garlic, mint, onions, oregano, parsley, sage, rosemary, or thyme
Poultry	Basil, curry, garlic, rosemary, sage, or thyme

Helpful Hints

After testing all the recipes in the book, we have learned quite a few tips and tricks. To give you a jump start, we've written up some of the tips that we have found most useful.

Shopping

▸ Make a list of ingredients before leaving home. This is a good idea for a couple of reasons: First, you won't forget anything, and second, you'll be less likely to add unnecessary and costly items to your cart.

▸ Check expiration dates. This is especially important for dairy, meat, and seafood products.

▸ Stores usually place fresher foods behind or under older items. It's okay to rummage a bit — don't make too much of a mess though.

▸ If you have a fish counter or a butcher in your supermarket, look at their specials. Fish and meats ordered there are likely to be fresher and sometimes less expensive than prepackaged items.

▸ Try to avoid buying chicken or fish on Sundays. Most supermarkets don't receive shipments over the weekend and don't clear away older produce, so you won't get the freshest product.

▸ Never buy dented cans. Dents increase the possibility of bacterial growth.

▸ When buying eggs, always open the carton and check each one to see that they aren't cracked or broken. Aside from being a waste of money and a mess, raw eggs can carry bacteria that you don't want smeared over everything else you've bought.

Cooking

▸ We've all learned that the easiest way to make mistakes is by not reading the instructions carefully. This includes cooking. Before you begin, read the entire recipe.

▸ When using a microwave oven, make sure that all items put inside are microwave-safe. Never use aluminum foil or anything that has metal on it in the microwave.

▸ Don't use clear plastic containers to reheat anything tomato-based in the microwave — you'll end up with all of your containers stained red. In fact, some health practitioners argue that, when microwaved, soft plastic containers leak toxic substances into the food they contain, so you may want to consider using just regular plates and bowls in the microwave.

▸ Make sure that there are no paper, plastic, or flammable items near the stove.

▸ When cooking on the stove top, never leave the handles of pots or pans turned outward. Turning the handles to the side eliminates the chance that you or hungry, impatient friends walking past the stove will accidentally knock them off.

- Always remember to stir, especially when reheating. If you don't, things that have settled on the bottom of the pot will burn.
- Always check twice to make sure the oven and stove are off — you don't want to burn the place down.

Freezing

- Label items before freezing. We guarantee that no matter how in touch you think you are with the contents of your freezer, at some point everything will begin to look the same.
- Think ahead and wrap up portions in the quantities you will want to prepare. For example, in order to save yourself the time and trouble of defrosting a whole block of ground beef, mold the beef into single-serving patties before freezing. This way you can defrost only what you need.
- Make sure that items placed in the freezer are wrapped well. Bags or containers need to be airtight to prevent freezer burn.
- Prepare all items exactly as you want them before freezing. For example, before freezing chicken, remove the fatty parts. You'll save yourself time later.

Defrosting

- Use a microwave for defrosting. It's simple and efficient. Make sure you remove any aluminum foil or plastic wrap first.
- Do not defrost any dish that, when fresh, needs to be refrigerated (such as dishes containing fish, poultry, or meat) by leaving it out at room temperature — keep it in the refrigerator. The outer parts, which defrost much more quickly than the inner parts, can easily go bad if left out.
- Plan ahead. If you're going to have to defrost something for dinner, take it out of the freezer the night or morning before and put it in the refrigerator. It will be defrosted, or at least mostly defrosted, by the time you want to cook it.
- Keep items that are defrosting on a plate. As they defrost, frozen foods leak water, which can make quite a mess if you don't prepare for it.
- Use cuts of fish, poultry, or meat within 24 hours of defrosting. Never refreeze these items.

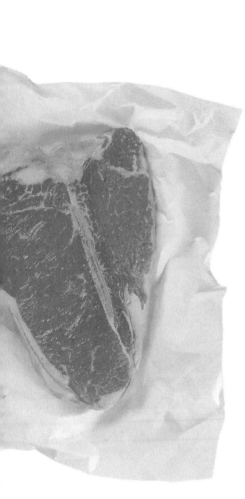

Reheating

▸ Using a microwave is probably the simplest way to reheat food. Remember to stir occasionally, since a microwave won't heat the food uniformly. If your microwave does not rotate the food while heating, be sure to do so yourself.

▸ When reheating on a stove top, use a low flame or low heat to maintain consistency and prevent burning. Stir frequently.

Handling Meats

▸ Always rinse raw poultry with cold water before using it.

▸ Try to minimize the amount of contact raw meat (including fish and poultry) has with anything in the kitchen, including countertops, cutting boards, knives, and plates. Wash those items thoroughly with hot water and soap before using them again.

▸ When preparing chicken and pork, you must make sure that they are completely cooked. This means no pink inside. When in doubt, cook longer.

▸ If you've bought a package of meat but you don't need all of it for your recipe, it's a good idea to cook it all anyway. You can always use the cooked meat in the next dish you prepare. If you don't cook it, freeze the remainder. It can spoil quickly if left in an open package in the refrigerator.

Cleaning Up

▸ Don't let dishes pile up. The longer you let it go, the harder it will be to get it done.

▸ Clean up as you go. While your dish is simmering, it doesn't require much of your attention. Use this opportunity to get a jump on the cleaning. Put spices back on the shelf. Wash the silverware, bowls, and pots you've used. Even though you may get them messy again, wipe down the counters — it's easier and more pleasant to cook in a clean kitchen. In addition to saving you time in the long run, you'll find it easier to motivate and do the less pleasant chores before you get full and slide into a food coma.

- If you have to clean an especially hard-to-scrub pan, first fill it with hot water and dishwashing soap and let it soak for a few hours.
- When cleaning dishes, use hot water. It helps to break down the oils.
- Always clean counters and stove tops after cooking. It's a two-minute task that makes the kitchen look a million times cleaner and will make cooking the next time a much more enjoyable experience.

Helpful Conversions

Although we have listed ingredients for our recipes in both standard (American) and metric measurements, we have found it convenient to have an index you can call on when cooking. In addition, the conversions listed here are also a breakdown of the units in the standard system. You will find in this section all the necessary information to convert a recipe into metric format or to halve any of the recipes in this book.

Weight

1 ounce = 28.5 grams
4 ounces = $^1/_4$ pound = 113 grams
8 ounces = $^1/_2$ pound = 225 grams
16 ounces = 1 pound = 450 grams

Volume

1 teaspoon = 5 ml
1 tablespoon = 3 teaspoons = 15 ml
$^1/_4$ cup = 4 tablespoons = 60 ml
$^1/_3$ cup = 5 tablespoons + 1 teaspoon = 80 ml
$^1/_2$ cup = 8 tablespoons = 125 ml
1 cup = 8 fluid ounces = 16 tablespoons = 250 ml
2 cups = 1 pint = 16 fluid ounces = 500 ml
4 cups = 2 pints = 1 quart = 32 fluid ounces = 1000 ml

Temperature

To quickly convert centigrade into Fahrenheit, multiply by 9, divide by 5, and add 32. To convert Fahrenheit into centigrade, subtract 32, multiply by 5, and divide by 9.

$$32°F = 0°C = \text{freezing point of water}$$
$$100°F = 38°C$$
$$212°F = 100°C = \text{boiling point of water}$$
$$325°F = 163°C$$
$$350°F = 177°C$$
$$375°F = 191°C$$
$$400°F = 204°C$$
$$425°F = 218°C$$
$$450°F = 232°C$$

Healthy Substitutions

We suggest these substitutions, especially in baking, to make your treats just a little bit lighter. Remember to use them in moderation — replacing all the oil and butter in a recipe with yogurt and applesauce will often leave you with a heavy brick. Use these substitutions wisely and you will find that you can't even tell the difference.

1 egg = 2 egg whites = $^{1}/_{4}$ cup egg substitute

1 unit butter or oil = 1 unit applesauce

1 unit butter or oil = 1 unit plain yogurt

1 unit mayonnaise = 1 unit plain yogurt

1 cup sour cream (in baking) = 1 cup milk + 1 tablespoon lemon
juice (let stand 5 minutes)

1 ounce cooking chocolate = 3 tablespoons hot chocolate powder +
1 tablespoon oil

1 slice chocolate cake = 27 minutes on the Stairmaster

Chapter 2

Champion Breakfasts

Everyone has heard that breakfast is the most important meal of the day. Breakfast kick-starts your metabolism, feeds your brain, and prepares you for what can often be a stressful and active day. Among college students, however, skipping breakfast still seems to be a contagious disease. If you find yourself all too often running out the door with a rumbling stomach, we suggest that you take a look at the following pages. Some of the recipes can even be prepared the night before for those days when you know you won't have much time.

You'll notice that we've included quite a few egg recipes here, and may wonder how those recipes qualify as "healthy." Although egg yolks are known to contain a high amount of cholesterol, their whites are full of protein and have no cholesterol or fat. There are also plenty of high quality, no-cholesterol egg substitutes that work just as well as the real thing. With eggs, you can make all sorts of elegant dishes that can be prepared quickly and cheaply such as omelettes, quiches, and frittatas. Avoid eating raw eggs — or taste-testing recipes that have raw eggs in them before they are cooked — as they can contain salmonella.

 Traditional Pancakes

Makes 3 servings, or about 9 pancakes

Mom's Tips

While You're Waiting

To keep pancakes warm while you finish preparing the remainder of the meal, stack them on a plate or baking dish in a 200°F (95°C) oven. Place a paper towel between pancakes to keep them from getting soggy.

This recipe works for all kinds of pancakes. Try mixing in blueberries, apples, peaches, or even chocolate chips. Save any leftovers, wrapped in plastic wrap, for a late-night snack or tomorrow's breakfast. One word of advice: When it comes to maple syrup, it's worthwhile to splurge. There's no substitute for the real thing.

1 cup (250 ml) all-purpose flour
½ teaspoon (3 ml) baking powder
2 tablespoons (30 ml) sugar
A pinch of salt

1 egg
1 cup (250 ml) skim milk
1 tablespoon (30 ml) vegetable oil
1 teaspoon (5 ml) vanilla
Cooking spray

1. In a medium bowl, combine the flour, baking powder, sugar, and salt.
2. In another bowl, mix together the egg, milk, oil, and vanilla. Add the dry ingredients and stir until the mixture is smooth.
3. Heat a nonstick skillet over medium heat until a drop of water dances on the surface and coat lightly with cooking spray. Pour in the batter in small puddles, one for each pancake. (If you don't have a nonstick skillet, you'll need to melt a little butter in the pan first to keep the pancakes from sticking.) Cook over medium heat until bubbles begin to appear and pop on the uncooked side. Flip and cook the other side. When both sides are golden brown, remove from pan.

★ Orange French Toast

Makes 4 servings

Serve each person two slices with orange-strawberry syrup poured over the top. If it's just you at the table, halve the recipe or save the leftovers for later.

1½ cups (375 ml) orange juice
2 eggs
¼ cup (60 ml) skim milk
¼ teaspoon (1 ml) cinnamon

½ teaspoon (3 ml) sugar
¼ cup (60 ml) strawberry jam
2 teaspoons (10 ml) butter
8 slices whole - wheat bread

Nutrition Per Serving	
Calories	253
Fat	8 g
Protein	12 g
Carbohydrates	63 g
Cholesterol	96 mg
Sodium	506 mg

1. In a bowl, combine ¹/₂ cup of the orange juice and the eggs, milk, cinnamon, and sugar. Set aside.

2. In a small saucepan, combine the remaining 1 cup of orange juice and the strawberry jam. Heat to a simmer, stirring until most of the jam is liquefied. Keep simmering over low heat.

3. In a large skillet over medium heat, melt about ¹/₄ of the butter. Dip bread (one piece at a time) in the egg mixture. Turn to coat both sides.

4. Cook each piece of bread in the skillet, flipping, until both sides are golden brown. Add more butter to the pan as necessary.

 # Orange Tofu Toast

Makes 2 servings

This recipes comes from a friend at Stanford University in California.

½ cup (125 ml) orange juice
1 teaspoon (5 ml) cinnamon
1 teaspoon (5 ml) sugar

¼ block tofu (¼ pound, or
113 g), sliced into thin strips
4 slices whole wheat bread

Nutrition Per Serving	
Calories	215
Fat	5 g
Protein	9 g
Carbohydrates	35 g
Cholesterol	35 mg
Sodium	274 mg

1. In a saucepan over medium heat, combine the orange juice, cinnamon, and sugar. When the mixture begins to bubble, add the strips of tofu. Cook for 3 minutes.

2. While the tofu is cooking, toast the bread.

3. Remove the tofu from the saucepan and lay the strips on the toast. Drizzle with juice from the pan.

# ★ Cold Fruit Cereal

Makes 2 servings

This is one of the best recipes you'll find for a quick breakfast.

Nutrition Per Serving	
Calories	210
Fat	1 g
Protein	8 g
Carbohydrates	44 g
Cholesterol	3 mg
Sodium	188 mg

¼ cup (60 ml) uncooked
quick oats
½ cup (125 ml) skim milk
¼ cup (60 ml) plain
nonfat yogurt

½ cup (125 ml) orange juice
1½ tablespoons (23 ml) honey
1 apple, chopped
¼ cup (60 ml) mixed fruit,
chopped (optional)

1. In a medium bowl, combine the oats, milk, and yogurt. Let stand for five minutes to allow the oats to soften.
2. Stir in the orange juice, honey, apples, and mixed fruit. Mix well. Serve cold.

Apple Oatmeal

Makes 2 servings

You can also try making variations of this recipe by substituting other fruits such as peaches, blueberries, or bananas, for the apple — just don't cook the softer fruits for as long.

Nutrition Per Serving	
Calories	158
Fat	1 g
Protein	6 g
Carbohydrates	32 g
Cholesterol	1 mg
Sodium	101 mg

½ cup (250 ml) rolled oats
(not the instant kind)
½ cup (250 ml) milk
½ cup (250 ml) water
2 tablespoons (30 ml) raisins

½ tablespoon (15 ml)
brown sugar
½ apple, chopped
A pinch of salt
Cinnamon for sprinkling

1. Mix together the oats, milk, water, raisins, brown sugar, apple, and salt in a saucepan. Bring to a boil, then cover, reduce heat, and let simmer for 10 minutes, stirring frequently.
2. When the mixture is thick and mushy, remove from heat. Sprinkle with cinnamon and serve.

 # Granola

Makes 20 servings

This recipe makes quite a bit of granola, which will keep for about a month when stored in an airtight container. We recommend sprinkling this mixture over yogurt and fruit.

- 3 cups (750 ml) rolled oats
- ½ cup (125 ml) sunflower seeds, shelled
- ½ cup (125 ml) pumpkin seeds
- ½ cup (125 ml) chopped walnuts
- ½ cup (125 ml) chopped almonds
- 3 tablespoons (45 ml) butter, melted
- 2 tablespoons (30 ml) vegetable oil
- 2 tablespoons (30 ml) molasses
- ¼ cup (60 ml) dark corn syrup

1. Preheat the oven to 400°F (205°C).
2. In a bowl, combine the oats, seeds, and nuts.
3. In a separate bowl, combine the remaining ingredients, stirring until well blended. Pour onto the oat mixture and mix well.
4. Spread the mixture in a shallow baking pan. Bake for about 15 minutes, stirring periodically, until it is dry.

KITCHEN QUICK TIP

In the Long Run

The recipe for granola may seem expensive when you go to buy the ingredients, but remember that it will keep for a long time in a sealed plastic container. Also keep in mind how expensive cereal is — in comparison, this recipe is a good deal *and* you're not eating all those artificial preservatives and sweeteners.

Hard-Boiled Egg

Makes 1 serving

Nutrition Per Serving

Calories	63
Fat	4 g
Protein	5 g
Carbohydrates	Less than 1 g
Cholesterol	181 mg
Sodium	54 mg

Many people have asked, "Just how healthy is an egg?" Well, we've broken it down for you here in the nutritional analysis of a hard-boiled egg, one of the quickest breakfasts or snacks you'll find. Remember, all of the fat and cholesterol live in the yolk.

1 egg

1. Place the egg in a pot and cover with water. Bring the water to a boil, then reduce heat and simmer for 13–15 minutes (depending on how well done you like them).
2. Using tongs, remove the egg from the water and immerse or rinse in cold water until it is cool enough to handle.

Poached Eggs

Makes 2 servings

Nutrition Per Serving

Calories	63
Fat	4 g
Protein	5 g
Carbohydrates	1 g
Cholesterol	183 mg
Sodium	54 mg

A custard dish is a small, round, ceramic or glass dish. You can often find them in grocery stores. For this recipe, however, any small dish that can be immersed in boiling water will do — just make sure that the sides are higher than the water level.

2 eggs
Salt and pepper to taste

1. Fill a pot with about 3 inches of water and bring to a boil. Lower heat to medium-high.
2. Crack an egg into a shallow custard dish. Slip the dish into the pot of boiling water. Don't worry if water spills in over the egg.
3. Cook for about 5 minutes, or until the egg is done to your satisfaction. Remove from the pot, using tongs, and sprinkle with salt and pepper.
4. Repeat steps 2 and 3 for the second egg.

# Scrambled Eggs

Makes 2 servings

To give the dish a twist, add some diced onions, peppers, or tomatoes.

1 teaspoon (5 ml) margarine
3 eggs

1 tablespoon (15 ml) skim milk
Salt and pepper to taste

Nutrition Per Serving	
Calories	115
Fat	8 g
Protein	8 g
Carbohydrates	1 g
Cholesterol	275 mg
Sodium	106 mg

1. Beat together the eggs and milk.
2. Melt the margarine in a skillet over low heat. Pour the egg mixture into the skillet, and season with salt and pepper.
3. Stir gently for 4–6 minutes. When finished, eggs should be soft and have no liquid remaining.

Frittata

Makes 1 serving

You're going to need a pan that can go straight under a broiler (like a pan with a metal handle) for this one.

2 tablespoons (30 ml) finely chopped onion
¼ cup (60 ml) chopped broccoli
2 mushrooms, sliced
½ teaspoon (3 ml) extra-virgin olive oil

2 eggs
1 teaspoon (5 ml) skim milk
A pinch of salt
Grated Parmesan cheese (optional)

Nutrition Per Serving	
Calories	171
Fat	11 g
Protein	12 g
Carbohydrates	6 g
Cholesterol	361 mg
Sodium	251 mg

1. Preheat the broiler.
2. In an ovenproof skillet over medium heat, sauté the vegetables in the olive oil until they soften. Remove from heat and set the vegetables aside, on a plate or in a bowl. Don't wash the pan yet.
3. Beat together the eggs, milk, and salt. Pour the egg mixture into the skillet, and stir slowly just until the bottom begins to get firm. Add the vegetables to the egg mixture, making sure that they are evenly dispersed.
4. Place the skillet under the broiler for about 5 minutes. The fritatta is done when its top is firm. Sprinkle with Parmesan cheese, if desired, and serve.

Tomato-Corn Spicy Omelette

Makes 2 servings

From a friend at Mount Holyoke College in South Hadley, Massachusetts. For those of you who need a kick to wake up in the morning, the hot sauce in this omelette may do the trick. Add another teaspoon if you need serious help. If you don't have a microwave in which to heat the vegetables and hot sauce, don't worry — just don't heat it up.

½ cup (125 ml) corn kernels
1 medium tomato, chopped
1 teaspoon (5 ml) hot sauce
4 eggs

¼ cup (60 ml) water
2 teaspoons (10 ml) butter
¼ cup (60 ml) shredded
   low-fat cheddar cheese

1. Combine the corn, tomato, and hot sauce in a small bowl and heat in the microwave on high for 1 minute. Set aside.
2. In a bowl, beat together the eggs and water.
3. Melt one teaspoon of the butter in a skillet over medium heat. Add half of the eggs and cook for 1–2 minutes, or until the edges begin to pull away from the pan and the middle begins to solidify.
4. Remove from heat and spoon half of the corn-tomato mixture on half of the omelette. Sprinkle with half of the shredded cheese and fold the eggs over the filling with a spatula. Return to heat for 30 more seconds, then carefully remove from the pan to a serving plate.
5. Repeat steps 3 and 4 with the remaining ingredients for a second omelette.

Note: This recipe can also be done completely in the microwave. Omit the butter and cook the eggs in a 9-inch pie plate for about 2 minutes on high in the microwave. If your microwave doesn't have a turntable, rotate the dish every 30 seconds. When the eggs are fully cooked, add the corn-tomato mixture and sprinkle with shredded cheese. Then fold the eggs over and heat for an additional 20 seconds.

⊕ Tomato-Basil Omelette

Makes 2 servings

A handful of chopped ripe tomatoes makes a wonderful addition to this recipe.

4 eggs
2 teaspoons (10 ml) butter
2 tablespoons (30 ml)
    tomato sauce

1 teaspoon (5 ml) dried basil
Salt and pepper to taste

1. Crack the eggs into a small bowl and beat them.
2. In a skillet over medium heat, melt one teaspoon of the butter. Add half of the eggs and cook for 1–2 minutes, or until the edges begin to pull away from the pan and the middle begins to solidify.
3. Spread half of the tomato sauce on one half of the omelette, sprinkle with half of the basil, then fold over. Season with salt and pepper; serve.
4. Repeat steps 2 and 3 with remaining ingredients.

Nutrition Per Serving	
Calories	162
Fat	12 g
Protein	11 g
Carbohydrates	1 g
Cholesterol	377 mg
Sodium	177 mg

★ Huevos Rancheros

Makes 2 servings

Here's one of our favorite recipes, which is just as good for lunch or dinner as it is for breakfast.

2 eggs
1 teaspoon (5 ml) skim milk
2 small flour tortillas
½ teaspoon (3 ml) butter

3 heaping tablespoons (45 ml)
    fat-free refried beans
Hot sauce to taste
1 tablespoon (15 ml) salsa

1. Beat together the eggs and milk.
2. Place the tortillas on the rack in a cold oven. Turn the oven to 300°F (180°C) and heat the tortillas for 5 minutes, or until warm and slightly crisp.
3. While the tortillas are warming, melt the butter in a small skillet over medium heat. Add the eggs, scramble, then transfer the eggs to a serving plate and place another plate upside down over them to keep them warm.
4. In the same skillet, heat the beans until warmed through.
5. Place the tortillas on fresh plates. Spread the beans over the tortillas, cover with eggs, sprinkle with hot sauce, and top with salsa.

Nutrition Per Serving	
Calories	190
Fat	7 g
Protein	10 g
Carbohydrates	25 g
Cholesterol	186 mg
Sodium	387 mg

Chapter 3

Appetizers & Quick Snacks

This section is a great resource if you are having company. Even though the recipes are quick and easy, your guests will think you've been in the kitchen for days. In addition, many of the appetizers included here are just dressy snacks, so if you are in the mood to munch, this is the chapter for you.

Quick snacks, on the other hand, are what you should be nibbling on instead of candy bars, potato chips, or microwave popcorn. Everyone can attest to the formidable nature of that sudden urge to snack. Most of these recipes don't take any longer to prepare than the time it would take you to dash down to a vending machine for a candy bar.

Guacamole

Makes 6 servings

Guacamole doesn't keep that well in the refrigerator — it tends to turn brown — so if you're making this recipe for just yourself, halve the ingredients. It's true that more than 80 percent of this recipe's calories comes from fat — that's from the avocado. However, the fat in avocados is unsaturated, not the saturated kind that doctors and nutritionists warn against, and not nearly as bad for you.

Nutrition Per Serving	
Calories	85
Fat	8 g
Protein	1 g
Carbohydrates	5 g
Cholesterol	0 mg
Sodium	185 mg

- 2 avocados, peeled and pitted
- 1 tablespoon (15 ml) lemon juice
- 2 tablespoons (30 ml) lime juice
- 1 tablespoon (15 ml) finely chopped onion
- 1 teaspoon (5 ml) salt
- ½ teaspoon (3 ml) chili powder
- Cayenne to taste
- 1 ripe jalapeño pepper, finely chopped (to reduce the heat, remove the seeds)
- 1 ripe tomato, chopped (optional)

1. Mash the avocados with a fork. If you like your guacamole extra smooth, puree it in a blender or food processor.
2. Add the remaining ingredients and mix well. Serve immediately with corn chips.

Nachos Supreme

Makes 6 servings

An all-time favorite on everyone's list. This is easy to make in the microwave as well. To bulk up these nachos, try adding some refried beans, cooked ground beef, chili, or green pepper. You can also try a variety of cheeses. The possibilities are endless.

Nutrition Per Serving	
Calories	158
Fat	5 g
Protein	8 g
Carbohydrates	21 g
Cholesterol	13 mg
Sodium	341 mg

- ½ of a 10-ounce (284 g) bag baked tortilla chips
- ¼ cup (60 ml) sliced black olives
- ¼ cup (60 ml) chopped onion
- ½ cup (125 ml) salsa
- 1 cup (250 ml) shredded low-fat cheddar cheese

1. Preheat the broiler.
2. Spread the tortilla chips evenly on a cookie sheet. Sprinkle with the olives and onion, then spoon salsa over all. Top with cheese.
3. Broil for about 2 minutes, or until the cheese is melted.

Roasted Red Pepper and Avocado Bites

Makes 8 servings

Nutrition Per Serving

Calories	157
Fat	7 g
Protein	9 g
Carbohydrates	17 g
Cholesterol	12 mg
Sodium	341 mg

Make only as much as you're planning to eat — this is one recipe that won't keep.

4 whole wheat English muffins
½ red onion, chopped
1 avocado, peeled, pitted, and sliced

1 roasted red pepper (see recipe on page 39)
1 cup (250 ml) shredded low-fat cheddar cheese
½ cup (60 ml) grated Parmesan cheese

1. Preheat the broiler. Split the muffins in half, place on a cookie sheet, and toast under the broiler for 2 minutes.
2. Place equal amounts of onion on the toasted muffins. Add one slice of avocado and one large piece of pepper to each. Top with equal amounts of cheddar cheese, then sprinkle with Parmesan.
3. Broil until the cheese is melted, about 2 minutes.

✒ ★ ① South of the Border Chip Dip

Makes 8 servings

This one gets a big star.

1 16-ounce (453 g) can
  fat-free refried beans
1 cup (250 ml) low-fat
  sour cream
1 tablespoon (15 ml) taco
  seasoning

1 cup (250 ml) salsa
1 cup (250 ml) shredded
  low-fat cheddar cheese
1 tomato, diced
¼ cup (60 ml) fresh cilantro
  leaves (optional)

Nutrition Per Serving	
Calories	131
Fat	4 g
Protein	8 g
Carbohydrates	15 g
Cholesterol	16 mg
Sodium	648 mg

1. Spread the beans evenly in a small casserole dish to form the bottom layer of the dip.
2. Mix together the sour cream and taco seasoning and then spread evenly over the beans. Top with the salsa.
3. Spread the cheese, tomato, and cilantro evenly over the salsa. Serve with tortilla chips as a party food.

Mom's Tips

Keeping Crackers

In humid weather, keep crackers and chips in an airtight container in the refrigerator to protect them from turning soft or soggy.

Deviled Eggs

Makes 6 servings

Refrigerate any leftovers, and be sure to eat them within 3 days of preparation.

Nutrition Per Serving

Calories	67
Fat	4 g
Protein	6 g
Carbohydrates	1 g
Cholesterol	183 mg
Sodium	82 mg

Nutrition Per Serving

Calories	67
Fat	4 g
Protein	6 g
Carbohydrates	1 g
Cholesterol	183 mg
Sodium	82 mg

- 6 hard-boiled eggs, peeled and halved lengthwise
- 3 tablespoons (45 ml) nonfat plain yogurt
- 1 tablespoon (15 ml) diced celery
- Salt and pepper to taste
- Curry powder to taste

1. Remove the yolks from the eggs.
2. Blend the yogurt, celery, and a pinch of salt with the yolks in a small bowl. Overfill each egg-white half with the yolk mixture.
3. Sprinkle the eggs with salt, pepper, and curry powder. Refrigerate until serving time.

Ants on a Log

Makes 4 servings

It seems that the older we get, the more we appreciate our childhood classics.

Nutrition Per Serving

Calories	48
Fat	3 g
Protein	2 g
Carbohydrates	4 g
Cholesterol	0 mg
Sodium	60 mg

- 4 stalks celery, trimmed and cleaned
- 1½ tablespoons (23 ml) peanut butter
- Raisins

1. Cut the celery into 2¹/₂-inch pieces. (Don't split the stalk — you'll need the trough in the center.)
2. Fill the trough with peanut butter, and top with raisins.

Mushrooms Parmesan

Makes 3 servings

When you remove the stems from the mushroom caps, make sure you get the whole stem, and that you're not just cracking the top off. There needs to be room for stuffing.

9 medium mushrooms
1 tablespoon (15 ml) butter

Grated Parmesan cheese to taste
Salt and pepper to taste

Nutrition Per Serving	
Calories	56
Fat	5 g
Protein	2 g
Carbohydrates	2 g
Cholesterol	12 mg
Sodium	80 mg

1. Preheat the broiler.
2. Wipe the mushrooms clean with a damp cloth. Pull the stems out of the mushroom caps. Place the caps upside down on a foil-lined cookie sheet.
3. Dice the mushroom stems and stuff them back into the caps. Place slivers of butter in the caps, and sprinkle the Parmesan cheese, salt, and pepper over each.
4. Broil for approximately 3 minutes, or until the mushrooms are light brown.

Italian Mushrooms

Makes 4 servings

Keep napkins handy when you serve this tasty but messy appetizer.

12 bite-size mushrooms
1½ cups (375 ml) Italian dressing (see page 130 for our own recipe)

1 tablespoon (15 ml) grated Parmesan cheese

Nutrition Per Serving	
Calories	82
Fat	7 g
Protein	2 g
Carbohydrates	3 g
Cholesterol	1 mg
Sodium	35 mg

1. Wipe the mushrooms clean with a damp cloth.
2. Place the mushrooms in a bowl and cover with the dressing. Add the cheese and stir well. Refrigerate for 2 hours.
3. Drain the dressing from the mushrooms, and serve with toothpicks.

Mustard-Horseradish Vegetable Dip

Makes 6 servings

This dip originally called for mayonnaise, but we used yogurt instead. Cut up various vegetables — we recommend carrots, broccoli, cauliflower, celery, and radishes — and serve beside the dip. Great for gatherings.

4 ½ tablespoons (68 ml) nonfat plain yogurt
5 teaspoons (25 ml) Dijon mustard

3 tablespoons (45 ml) horseradish

Combine all the ingredients and mix well. Serve immediately.

Artichoke Dip

Makes 8 servings

This classic dip is traditionally high in calories, but we've made some simple substitutions to make it more healthy.

1 15-ounce (425 g) can artichoke hearts in water, drained
¼ cup (60 ml) low-fat mayonnaise
¼ cup (60 ml) nonfat plain yogurt

½ cup (125 ml) grated Parmesan cheese
¼ teaspoon (1 ml) pepper
1 teaspoon (5 ml) chopped parsley (optional)

1. Preheat the oven to 400°F (205°C).
2. Drain the artichoke hearts and chop coarsely.
3. Combine the artichoke hearts with the mayonnaise, yogurt, cheese, and pepper; mix thoroughly. Spread evenly in a small casserole dish or loaf pan.
4. Bake for 20 minutes, or until hot and lightly brown. Remove from the oven, top with parsley, and serve with crackers or sliced French bread rounds.

Baked Garlic

Makes 6 servings

When baked, garlic becomes as soft and spreadable as butter. It's fantastic spread on French bread, topped with tomato, and seasoned with a little salt and pepper. You can also try it on crackers, in sandwiches, or as a topping for vegetables.

1 whole bulb garlic

1. Preheat the oven to 400°F (205°C).
2. Remove the papery outer leaves of the garlic bulb. Cut off the stem end of the bulb so that each clove is open at the top.
3. Set the bulb in a pan or on a baking sheet. Bake for 45 minutes. Garlic is finished when the cloves are tender and the husks are golden brown. Serve with warm French bread.

Note: You can also bake garlic in the microwave. Cook on high for 1–1$^1/_2$ minutes

Nutrition Per Serving	
Calories	21
Fat	2 g
Protein	0 g
Carbohydrates	0 g
Cholesterol	0 mg
Sodium	1 mg

Roasted Red Pepper

Makes 1 serving

Roasted red peppers are most commonly enjoyed in sandwiches or on salads.

1 red pepper

1. Preheat the oven to 350°F (180°C).
2. Line a baking pan with aluminum foil. Place the pepper in the pan and bake for 30 minutes, turning it occasionally.
3. Remove the pepper from the oven and place it in a plastic bag. Then seal the bag shut.
4. When the pepper is cool enough to handle, remove it from the bag and peel off its skin. Cut it open and remove the seeds, then slice the flesh into long strips.

Nutrition Per Serving	
Calories	20
Fat	0 g
Protein	1 g
Carbohydrates	5 g
Cholesterol	0 mg
Sodium	1 mg

★ Your Basic Hummus

Makes 10 servings

Nutrition Per Serving

Calories	92
Fat	4 g
Protein	3 g
Carbohydrates	12 g
Cholesterol	0 mg
Sodium	128 mg

This recipe comes from a friend at Vanderbilt University in Nashville, Tennessee. Great for sandwiches, bagels, and dipping, hummus is an all-purpose food. You'll need a food processor to make it.

- 1 15-ounce (425 g) can chickpeas (also known as garbanzo beans)
- 2 cloves fresh garlic, minced
- ¼ cup (60 ml) sesame tahini
- ⅓ cup (80 ml) lemon juice
- ¼ teaspoon (1 ml) cayenne

1. Drain the chickpeas, saving the juice. Dump the beans into the food processor.
2. Add the remaining ingredients and blend until smooth. If the mixture is too thick add some of the bean juice; blend until it reaches the desired consistency.

★ ◷ Hummus Sandwich

Makes 1 serving

Nutrition Per Serving

Calories	447
Fat	6 g
Protein	21 g
Carbohydrates	88 g
Cholesterol	0 mg
Sodium	286 mg

To keep the pita pocket from cracking when you split it open, try heating it first in the microwave for [five to ten] seconds.

- 2 heaping tablespoons (45 ml) hummus (store-bought, or see our recipe above)
- ½ pita pocket
- 4 slices cucumber
- Handful of bean sprouts
- Chopped vegetables of your choice — try green or red pepper, carrots, or red onions (optional)

Spread the hummus in the pita pocket. Slide in the cucumber slices, sprouts, and any other vegetables you may be using.

Vegetable Cream Cheese

Makes 8 servings

Refrigerate and save for bagel topping.

1 8-ounce (227 g) tub nonfat cream cheese

1 tablespoon (15 ml) sliced scallions

1 teaspoon (5 ml) finely diced carrot

1 teaspoon (5 ml) finely diced green or red pepper

1. In a mixing bowl, combine all the ingredients. Mix thoroughly.
2. Spoon the cream cheese back into its tub (or another container) and refrigerate.

Nutrition Per Serving	
Calories	26
Fat	0 g
Protein	4 g
Carbohydrates	1 g
Cholesterol	5 mg
Sodium	170 mg

Gourmet Endives

Makes 8 servings

This recipe comes compliments of a friend at Harvard University in Cambridge, Massachusetts. It's simple, elegant, and delicious.

5 tablespoons (75 ml) low-fat cream cheese

1 tablespoon (15 ml) dried oregano

1 teaspoon (5 ml) dried basil

¼ teaspoon (1 ml) salt

¼ teaspoon (1 ml) pepper

3 endives

1. In a small bowl, combine the cream cheese with the oregano, basil, salt, and pepper, and mix thoroughly.
2. Separate the endive leaves and arrange them on a plate. Spread the cream cheese into the troughs.

Nutrition Per Serving	
Calories	51
Fat	2 g
Protein	3 g
Carbohydrates	6 g
Cholesterol	5 mg
Sodium	165 mg

 # Quesadillas

Makes 4 servings

Nutrition Per Serving

Calories	179
Fat	6 g
Protein	9 g
Carbohydrates	21 g
Cholesterol	15 mg
Sodium	272 mg

Any of the tortilla fillings recommended below would also make a great addition to a quesadilla.

¾ cup (185 ml) shredded low-fat cheddar cheese
½ tomato, diced

2 medium mushrooms, diced
¼ onion, diced
4 flour tortillas

1. Preheat the oven to 350°F (180°C).
2. Combine the cheese, tomato, mushroom, and onion in a small bowl.
3. Place the tortillas on a cookie sheet. Spread ¼ of the cheese mixture over half of each tortilla.
4. Bake for 7 minutes, or until the cheese is bubbling. Remove from the oven. Fold the bare half of each tortilla over the filled half. Serve warm.

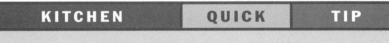

KITCHEN QUICK TIP

6 Quick Fillings for a Tortilla

▸ Refried beans, tomato, and cheese
▸ Black beans, corn, and cinnamon
▸ Grilled or sautéed vegetables with sour cream — onions, peppers, zucchini, eggplant, or whatever's lingering in the refrigerator
▸ Cottage cheese and salsa
▸ Tomato, avocado, and lemon or lime juice
▸ Leftover chicken or beef, salsa, and sour cream

Grilled Cheese and Tomato Sandwich

Makes 1 serving

A classic. Best served with tomato soup.

1 slice low-fat cheddar
cheese
2 slices whole wheat bread

1 slice tomato
Basil to taste
1 teaspoon (5 ml) butter

1. Lay the cheese on one slice of bread. Top with the tomato, basil, and the second slice of bread.
2. In a small skillet over medium-high heat, melt the butter. Cook the sandwich for about 2 minutes per side, or until the cheese is melted and the bread is golden brown.

Nutrition Per Serving	
Calories	320
Fat	12 g
Protein	16 g
Carbohydrates	40 g
Cholesterol	30 mg
Sodium	621 mg

Tomato and Pesto Sandwich

Makes 1 serving

This one is terrific and especially easy if you have a little leftover pesto.

½ tablespoon (8 ml) pesto
2 slices toast

2 slices tomato

Spread the pesto on one side of one slice of toast. Top with the tomato and the second slice of toast. Serve.

Nutrition Per Serving	
Calories	171
Fat	5 g
Protein	5 g
Carbohydrates	25 g
Cholesterol	3 mg
Sodium	321 mg

The Chagel

Makes 1 serving

Nutrition Per Serving

Calories	274
Fat	7 g
Protein	15 g
Carbohydrates	39 g
Cholesterol	184 mg
Sodium	470 mg

This recipe comes from a friend at the University of Pennsylvania. If you don't have a microwave, you can melt the cheese in a broiler — remember to preheat it.

1 egg, beaten
1 bagel of choice, toasted
1 tablespoon (15 ml) shredded low-fat mozzarella cheese

Salt, pepper, and cayenne to taste

1. Heat a nonstick skillet over medium heat. Add the egg and cook, stirring gently, until firm and dry.
2. While the egg is cooking, slice and toast the bagel.
3. Spoon the egg onto one bagel half. Sprinkle the cheese on top and heat in the microwave (or broil) until the cheese is melted. Season with salt, pepper, and cayenne. Close like a sandwich and enjoy.

English Muffin Pizza

Makes 2 servings

Nutrition Per Serving

Calories	116
Fat	3 g
Protein	6g
Carbohydrates	15 g
Cholesterol	8 mg
Sodium	338 mg

This recipe is even easier to prepare in a toaster oven.

2 tablespoons (15 ml) tomato sauce
1 English muffin, split in half
Oregano to taste

¼ cup (60 ml) shredded low-fat mozzarella cheese
2 black olives, sliced

1. Preheat the oven to 350°F (180°C).
2. Spread the tomato sauce evenly over the English muffin halves. Sprinkle with oregano and cheese. Top with the olives.
3. Place on a cookie sheet and bake for 5 minutes, or until the cheese is melted.

Onion Pizza

Makes 1 serving

Try seasoning this recipe with basil, oregano, or black pepper.

Nutrition Per Serving	
Calories	372
Fat	8 g
Protein	14 g
Carbohydrates	40 g
Cholesterol	16 mg
Sodium	516 mg

1 tablespoon (15 ml) tomato sauce
1 small ready-made pizza crust
1 slice red onion, chopped
¼ cup (60 ml) shredded lowfat mozzarella cheese

1. Preheat the broiler.
2. Spread the tomato sauce over the pizza crust. Sprinkle with onion and cover with cheese, spreading evenly.
3. Broil for about 2 minutes, or until the cheese has melted.

Quick Western Sandwich

Makes 1 serving

This is another recipe that's great with whatever vegetables — peppers, tomatoes, onions, zucchini — you have hanging out in the refrigerator.

Nutrition Per Serving	
Calories	307
Fat	10 g
Protein	16 g
Carbohydrates	41 g
Cholesterol	187 mg
Sodium	584 mg

½ teaspoon (3 ml) butter
1 egg, beaten
2 tablespoons (30 ml) sliced green onion
1 tablespoon (15 ml) shredded nonfat mozzarella cheese
1 teaspoon (5 ml) hot sauce (optional)
2 slices whole wheat bread

1. Heat the butter in a large skillet over medium-high heat. Add the egg, onion, cheese, and hot sauce. Cook, stirring gently for 2–3 minutes or until firm and dry.
2. While the egg mixture cooks, toast the two slices of bread.
3. Place the egg and onion mixture on one slice of toast and top with the second slice. Cut the sandwich in two and serve immediately.

Cottage Cheese on a Bagel

Makes 1 serving

Try this instead of cream cheese!

Nutrition Per Serving

Calories	121
Fat	Less than 1 g
Protein	7 g
Carbohydrates	20 g
Cholesterol	1 mg
Sodium	264 mg

½ bagel
2 tablespoons (30 ml) fat-free cottage cheese
Cinnamon and sugar to taste

1. Toast the bagel.
2. Top the toasted bagel with cottage cheese, and sprinkle with cinnamon and sugar.

Tuna Melt

Makes 4 servings

If you have one, prepare this quick snack in a toaster oven.

Nutrition Per Serving

Calories	151
Fat	4 g
Protein	15 g
Carbohydrates	14 g
Cholesterol	20 mg
Sodium	337 mg

2 English muffins, split in half
1 6-ounce (170 g) can tuna in water, drained
1½ tablespoons (23 ml) low-fat mayonnaise

Salt and pepper to taste
¼ cup (60 ml) shredded low-fat cheddar cheese

1. Preheat the oven to 350°F (180°C). Toast the muffins.
2. Mix the tuna, mayonnaise, salt, and pepper. Place ¼ of the mixture on each English muffin half. Press with a fork to flatten. Sprinkle the cheese evenly over the tops of the muffins.
3. Bake until the cheese is melted, about 5 minutes.

 # Honey Butter

Makes 6 servings

This is a great spread to serve over toast, English muffins, or pancakes — the extra flavor allows you to use it in moderation.

> **2 tablespoons (30 ml) butter**
> **2 tablespoons (30 ml) honey**
> **1 teaspoon (5 ml) vanilla**

Nutrition Per Serving	
Calories	57
Fat	4 g
Protein	0 g
Carbohydrates	6 g
Cholesterol	10 mg
Sodium	39 mg

1. In a small saucepan warm the butter slightly. Add the honey and vanilla, and mix well.

2. Use immediately or refrigerate for later.

 # Banana Shake

Makes 1 serving

This shake is also good with other fruits.

> **¾ cup fruit-flavored nonfat yogurt**
> **1 teaspoon (5 ml) honey**
> **1 small banana**
> **¼ cup (80 ml) skim milk**
> **A pinch of cinnamon**

Nutrition Per Serving	
Calories	190
Fat	Less than 1 g
Protein	7 g
Carbohydrates	42 g
Cholesterol	3 mg
Sodium	87 mg

Combine all the ingredients in a blender and process until smooth.

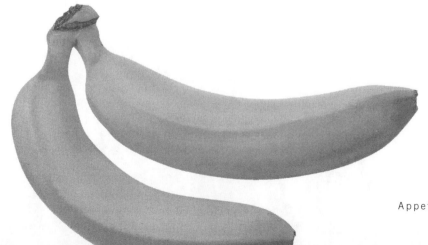

Chapter 4

Soups & Salads

Soups and salads are terrific and versatile dishes. Either one can be eaten as a prelude to a fancy dinner, as a healthy snack, or as a meal in itself. While hot soup is especially appreciated on cold winter evenings, we also have some chilled varieties, which provide a refreshing touch on warmer days. Keep in mind that soups often can be frozen and kept for another time, so it's a good idea to make extra for quick meals throughout the week.

As for salads, while iceberg lettuce with oil and vinegar is always an option, there are many more interesting combinations out there that deserve a try. They range from greens to pasta to fruit, and even to tofu for the more adventurous at heart. Many of the suggestions offered in this section are as good for large gatherings as they are for dinner for one. Many can also be refrigerated and stored for an easy snack or for dinner tomorrow evening. Don't worry if you don't have all of the vegetables that any recipe calls for — just use what you have and see how things turn out. You may even like your new salad better.

Try mixing and matching vinaigrettes and dressings with different types of salads. We've included a number of recipes for homemade dressings, all of which are listed on pages 129–131 in chapter 10.

Bean and Tomato Soup

Makes 4 servings

This could be the world's easiest soup to make — and it tastes good. It doesn't matter what size cans of tomatoes, beans, and broth you use as long as all three cans are the same size.

1 can whole stewed tomatoes, drained and cut into bite-size pieces
1 can kidney beans, drained

1 can low-sodium vegetable broth
½ clove garlic, finely chopped
A dash of pepper

Nutrition Per Serving	
Calories	390
Fat	1 g
Protein	29 g
Carbohydrates	82 g
Cholesterol	0 mg
Sodium	516 mg

1. Combine the contents of the three cans in a saucepan. Bring the mixture to a boil, then add the garlic and pepper. Reduce heat and simmer for 10 minutes.
2. Pour half the mixture into a blender and process until smooth. Return the mixture to the pot, mix well, and serve.

Cucumber Dill Soup

Makes 4 servings

This cold soup makes a good complement to spicy dishes.

4 medium cucumbers
2 cups (500 ml) nonfat plain yogurt

2 tablespoons (30 ml) fresh dill
½ teaspoon (3 ml) salt
1 teaspoon lemon juice

Nutrition Per Serving	
Calories	140
Fat	1 g
Protein	11 g
Carbohydrates	25 g
Cholesterol	2 mg
Sodium	365 mg

1. Slice the cucumbers lengthwise. Scoop out and discard the seeds, then slice into rounds.
2. Process all the ingredients in a blender until smooth.
3. Refrigerate for 30 minutes. Serve cold.

Egg Drop Soup

Makes 6 servings

Tastes just like what's served at Chinese restaurants.

Nutrition Per Serving

Calories	45
Fat	2 g
Protein	10 g
Carbohydrates	2 g
Cholesterol	90 mg
Sodium	372 mg

4 cups (1 l) low-sodium chicken broth
2 cups (500 ml) water
1 teaspoon (5 ml) powdered ginger

3 eggs, beaten
1 tablespoon (15 ml) sliced scallions

1. In a medium pot, combine the broth, water, and ginger. Bring to a boil.

2. Stir in the beaten eggs and scallions and cook for one minute longer. Serve hot.

★ Potato-Leek Soup

Makes 6 servings

This soup is a unanimous favorite and a great hit with all of our friends. It's also good served with a sprinkle of Parmesan cheese. Be sure to clean your leeks thoroughly — grit often gets caught between the layers. Also, use only the light-colored part of the leek; the green part is tough and not as flavorful.

Nutrition Per Serving

Calories	129
Fat	Less than 1 g
Protein	3 g
Carbohydrates	30 g
Cholesterol	0 mg
Sodium	380 mg

3 medium potatoes, scrubbed, peeled, and cut into bite-size pieces
3 cups (750 ml) chopped leeks (three or four large ones)

2 tablespoons (30 ml) finely chopped chives
2 medium carrots, chopped
4 cups (1 l) water
1 teaspoon (5 ml) salt
Pepper to taste

1. Place the potatoes, leeks, chives, carrots, water, and salt in a large pot. Bring to a boil, reduce heat, and simmer for 20 minutes, or until the potatoes are tender. Remove from heat and allow contents to cool until the pot is comfortable to handle.

2. Transfer the soup to a blender or food processor and puree. Return the soup to the pot and heat. Season with pepper and serve hot.

Zucchini-Broccoli Soup

Makes 4 servings

For a vegetarian variety, use vegetable bouillon instead of chicken.

1⅓ cups (330 ml) water
2 medium zucchini, sliced
1½ cups (375 ml) chopped
broccoli

½ teaspoon (3 ml) minced
garlic
2 cubes chicken bouillon
A dash of pepper

1. Heat the water in a saucepan. Add the zucchini and broccoli and steam until soft. Reserve the leftover water.
2. Drop the bouillon cubes into the leftover water and stir until dissolved.
3. In a blender, puree all the ingredients (including bouillon broth) until smooth.

Mom's Tips

Quick & Easy Vegetables

To steam any kind of fresh vegetable, first chop it up into whatever size you prefer. Place it in a steamer basket or a stainless-steel colander that will fit inside a pot and fill the pot with an inch or two of water (so that it doesn't cover any of the vegetable). If you don't have a steamer or colander, you can place the vegetables right in the pot and fill it with just ¼ to ½ inch of water. Bring to a boil, reduce heat, and then simmer until the vegetables are tender. Different vegetables take different amounts of time — squash, for example, takes only a minute, while broccoli takes a couple of minutes and string beans take about five minutes.

Black Bean Onion Soup

Makes 8 servings

You can also make this recipe with dried beans — just cook them according to the package instructions.

2 medium onions, chopped
3 cloves garlic, minced
1 tablespoon (15 ml) canola oil
5½ cups (1375 ml) cooked black beans (approximately 4 15-ounce [254 g] cans)

7 cups (1.75 l) water
1 cup (250 ml) chopped green pepper
Salt and pepper to taste
Shredded cheddar cheese (optional)

1. In a medium skillet over medium heat, sauté the onion and garlic in the oil until soft (about 7 minutes).
2. Combine the onion and garlic in a large pot with the beans and water. Bring to a boil.
3. Add the green pepper. Reduce heat and simmer for 10 minutes.
4. Allow to cool slightly and then puree half of the soup in a blender. Return mixture to the pot and heat to serving temperature. Top with cheese, if desired, and serve.

 # ★ Lentil-Corn Soup

Makes 8 servings

This recipe takes about an hour to prepare, but most of your work will simply entail keeping an eye on the pot.

Nutrition Per Serving	
Calories	133
Fat	1 g
Protein	9 g
Carbohydrates	25 g
Cholesterol	0 mg
Sodium	413 mg

1 cup (250 ml) dried lentils, rinsed
4 cups (1 l) water
1 medium onion, chopped
2 cups (500 ml) chopped tomatoes, fresh or canned

2 cups (500 ml) corn kernels, fresh or frozen
1 teaspoon (5 ml) dried basil
3 cloves garlic, minced
1½ teaspoons (8 ml) salt

1. Combine the lentils and water in a large pot. Bring to a boil, reduce heat, and simmer for 30–40 minutes, or until the lentils are soft.
2. Add the remaining ingredients, and simmer for another 20 minutes.

Gazpacho

Makes 6 servings

Although this recipe has many ingredients, it takes only about 20 minutes to make. If you prefer smooth gazpacho, rather than chunky, simply puree the finished recipe.

Nutrition Per Serving	
Calories	47
Fat	Less than 1 g
Protein	4 g
Carbohydrates	18 g
Cholesterol	1 mg
Sodium	825 mg

2 cups (500 ml) low-sodium vegetable broth
2 cups (500 ml) tomato juice
2 tablespoons (30 ml) lemon juice
½ teaspoon (3 ml) hot sauce
1 clove garlic, minced

1 teaspoon (5 ml) salt
1 green pepper, chopped
1 cucumber, peeled, seeded, and chopped
4 medium tomatoes, chopped
1 onion, chopped

1. In a large pot, combine the broth, tomato juice, lemon juice, hot sauce, garlic, and salt. Cook, uncovered, over medium heat, until the mixture comes to a boil.
2. Add the vegetables. Return to a boil, reduce heat, and let simmer for 2 minutes. Remove from heat.
3. Cover and refrigerate. Serve cold.

★ Mama Bahr's Carrot Soup

Makes 4 servings

This soup is terrific, hot or cold.

Nutrition Per Serving	
Calories	155
Fat	6 g
Protein	13 g
Carbohydrates	22 g
Cholesterol	16 mg
Sodium	650 mg

2 tablespoons (30 ml) butter
½ large onion, minced
1½ tablespoons (23 ml) tomato paste
¼ cup (60 ml) uncooked rice
4 cups (1 l) low-sodium chicken broth

¾ of a 1-pound (454 g) bag of carrots, peeled and chopped
Salt and pepper to taste

1. Melt the butter in a large pot over medium heat. Sauté the onion in butter until transparent.
2. Add the tomato paste, rice, chicken broth, and carrots to the sautéed onion. Bring to a boil, reduce heat, and simmer until carrots are soft (about 45 minutes).
3. Puree the soup in a blender or food processor. (You may need to do it in a couple of batches.) Season with salt and pepper. Serve hot or cold.

Mom's Tips

Cooking with Broth

▸ When an otherwise all-vegetable recipe calls for beef or chicken broth, you can substitute vegetable broth to make the recipe vegetarian.
▸ Many canned broths and bouillon cubes are extremely high in sodium, so when you're shopping, be sure to look for the low-sodium varieties.

# Mushroom-Barley Soup

Makes 6 servings

Barley is a tasty and healthy grain. You can find it in the grains section of any grocery store.

1 tablespoon (15 ml) butter
½ large yellow onion, finely chopped
1 small carrot, finely chopped
1 small celery stalk, finely chopped
15 medium white mushrooms, chopped

5 cups (1.25 l) low-sodium chicken, beef, or vegetable broth
1 cup (250 ml) pearl barley (rinsed)
Salt and pepper to taste

Nutrition Per Serving	
Calories	170
Fat	3 g
Protein	14 g
Carbohydrates	32 g
Cholesterol	5 mg
Sodium	465 mg

1. Melt the butter in a large pot over medium heat. Add the onion, carrot, and celery and sauté until the onion becomes translucent. Add the mushrooms and cook until they begin to soften.
2. Add the broth and barley to the sautéed vegetables. Bring to a boil, reduce heat, and simmer for 50–60 minutes, or until the barley is fully hydrated. Season with salt and pepper.

Onion Soup

Makes 6 servings

An elegant and incredibly cheap soup. We recommend serving it with a slice of toasted French bread topped with Gruyère cheese floating in the bowl.

3 medium onions, thinly sliced
2 tablespoons (30 ml) butter

6 cups (1.5 l) low-sodium chicken broth
¼ teaspoon (1 ml) pepper

1. Warm the butter in a large pot over medium heat. Add the onions and sauté until they are well browned.
2. Add the broth and pepper. Bring the mixture to a boil, reduce heat, and let simmer for 20 minutes. Serve hot.

Mom's Tips

Saving Soup

Freezing soup is a great way to plan for the upcoming week. However, don't fill the container to the brim. As soup freezes it will expand, so you'll need to leave some headroom.

Nutrition Per Serving	
Calories	79
Fat	4 g
Protein	12 g
Carbohydrates	8 g
Cholesterol	10 mg
Sodium	559 mg

⏱ Quick Chicken Soup

Makes 3 servings

Nutrition Per Serving

Calories	125
Fat	2 g
Protein	19 g
Carbohydrates	6 g
Cholesterol	49 mg
Sodium	1,229 mg

This soup is a great way to use up leftover chicken. If you prefer an even heartier soup, try adding some rice or pasta — if uncooked, add with other ingredients in step 1 to boiling water; if already cooked, add 5 minutes before the soup is done cooking.

3 cups (750 ml) water
3 chicken bouillon
  cubes
2 carrots, sliced

2 celery stalks, chopped
1 cup (250 ml) chopped
  chicken (optional; included
  in nutritional information)

1. In a saucepan, bring the water to a boil and add the bouillon cubes, carrots, and celery. Reduce heat and let simmer for 10 minutes, or until the carrots become soft.
2. Add the chopped chicken and let simmer for 2 minutes more.

🫛 Quick Veggie Soup

Makes 4 servings

Nutrition Per Serving

Calories	97
Fat	2 g
Protein	11 g
Carbohydrates	18 g
Cholesterol	4 mg
Sodium	442 mg

This soup could not be any easier to make, but the best part about it is its versatility. Although it works best if you can include some carrot or potato, use whatever vegetables you have on hand.

1 yellow onion, chopped
1 cup (250 ml) chopped carrots
½ tablespoon (8 ml) butter
3 cups (750 ml) low-sodium
  chicken broth

½ cup (125 ml) chopped celery
1 cup (250 ml) chopped broccoli
½ baking potato, chopped
½ teaspoon (3 ml) dried oregano
Salt and pepper to taste

1. Melt the butter in a large pot over medium heat. Add the onion and carrots and sauté until the onion becomes translucent.
2. Add the broth, celery, broccoli, potato, and spices. Bring to a boil, reduce heat, and simmer for 20 minutes.

Basic Green Salad

Makes 4 servings

This is as basic as it comes. Try adding whatever chopped vegetables, sprouts, and herbs you prefer.

½ **head of lettuce (try using more than one variety)**

1 **plump tomato, sliced**
⅓ **red onion, thinly sliced**

1. Wash, dry, and chop the lettuce. Place in a serving bowl and top with the tomato and onion.
2. Serve with your favorite dressing.

Nutrition Per Serving	
Calories	13
Fat	Less than 1 g
Protein	1 g
Carbohydrates	3 g
Cholesterol	0 mg
Sodium	4 mg

Mediterranean Salad

Makes 4 servings

For an easy, at-home version of the Mediterranean.

1 **large tomato, chopped**
½ **cucumber, halved length-wise and sliced**
¾ **cup (185 ml) shredded low-fat mozzarella cheese**
¼ **cup (60 ml) olives, pitted and halved**

¾ **of a 15-ounce (425 g) can chickpeas, drained**
¼ **cup (80 ml) low-calorie Italian dressing (see page 130 for our recipe)**
Oregano to taste

1. In a medium bowl, combine the tomato, cucumber, cheese, olives, and chickpeas.
2. Add the dressing and toss lightly. Sprinkle with oregano.

Nutrition Per Serving	
Calories	201
Fat	8 g
Protein	11 g
Carbohydrates	23 g
Cholesterol	16 mg
Sodium	590 mg

 # Greek Salad

Makes 4 servings

Nutrition Per Serving

Calories	133
Fat	10 g
Protein	3 g
Carbohydrates	10 g
Cholesterol	6 mg
Sodium	185 mg

This recipe, from Smith College in Northampton, Massachusetts, makes a substantial salad that can often pass as a meal.

2 heads romaine lettuce
½ red onion, chopped
1 cucumber, chopped
1 green pepper, seeded and chopped
1 tomato, cut into wedges
¼ cup (60 ml) crumbled feta cheese
⅓ cup sliced black olives
2 tablespoons (30 ml) extra-virgin olive oil

2 tablespoons (30 ml) lemon juice
1 tablespoon (15 ml) red wine vinegar
1 clove garlic, minced
1 teaspoon (5 ml) chopped fresh oregano (or ½ teaspoon dried)
Salt and pepper to taste

1. In a large bowl, toss together the lettuce, onion, cucumber, green pepper, tomato, feta, and olives.
2. In a separate bowl, whisk together the olive oil, lemon juice, vinegar, garlic, oregano, salt, and pepper.
3. Pour the dressing over the salad and toss. Serve immediately.

Mom's Tips

Making Croutons

Make your own croutons for salads by cutting French bread into small cubes. Dry the cubes on a cookie sheet in a 200°F (95°C) oven until they are brown and crunchy. It's a great way to use up bread that's going stale.

★Roasted Red Pepper and Feta Salad

Makes 4 servings

Substitute tomatoes for the roasted red peppers to provide an equally tasty salad.

1 **roasted red pepper, chopped (see page 39 for directions)**
½ **cup (185 ml) crumbled feta cheese**

Oregano to taste
½ **head lettuce, washed and chopped**

Combine the pepper with the cheese, tossing to mix. Season with oregano. Serve on a bed of lettuce.

Nutrition Per Serving	
Calories	50
Fat	3 g
Protein	3 g
Carbohydrates	3 g
Cholesterol	13 mg
Sodium	16 mg

★① Tomato, Basil, and Mozzarella Salad

Makes 4 servings

Save this recipe for the summertime, when tomatoes are at their ripest, best flavor.

4 **slices tomato**
4 **leaves fresh basil**
4 **slices low-fat mozzarella**

Freshly ground black pepper to taste

Place the tomatoes on a plate. Top with the basil leaves and mozzarella and season with black pepper.

Nutrition Per Serving	
Calories	20
Fat	1 g
Protein	2 g
Carbohydrates	0 g
Cholesterol	4 mg
Sodium	37 mg

★ Taco Salad

Makes 4 servings

This is a hearty salad, and can be eaten as a meal.

½ pound (225 g) lean
   ground beef
Cayenne to taste
Chili powder to taste
Salt and pepper to taste
24 baked corn chips
¼ head lettuce, shredded

1 tomato, sliced
¼ green pepper, finely
   chopped
3 tablespoons (45 ml) finely
   chopped red onion
⅓ cup (80 ml) salsa
4 olives, thinly sliced

1. In a small skillet over medium heat, brown the beef. Season with the spices.
2. Line the edges of four servings bowls with the chips. Add the lettuce and top with the meat, followed by the tomato, green pepper, onion, a dollop of salsa, and sliced olives.

Bean and Corn Salad

Makes 4 servings

A good side dish for Mexican meals.

1½ cups (375 ml) dried black
   beans, soaked for 6 hours
   or overnight
1 cup (250 ml) cooked corn

½ cup (125 ml) thinly sliced
   red onion
1 fresh tomato, diced
2 tablespoons (30 ml) cider
   vinegar

In a large mixing bowl, combine all the ingredients. Cover and refrigerate. Serve chilled.

Potato Salad

Makes 4 servings

The skin of a potato contains quite a bit of its nutritional value. So don't peel your potatoes before cooking them unless the skin is particularly thick — you'll be throwing away the best part of the meal.

Nutrition Per Serving

Calories	90
Fat	1 g
Protein	2 g
Carbohydrates	19 g
Cholesterol	0 mg
Sodium	275 mg

- 4 medium red potatoes, washed
- ¼ cup (60 ml) red wine vinegar
- 2 tablespoons (30 ml) water
- 1 teaspoon lemon juice
- 1 teaspoon (5 ml) extra-virgin olive oil
- 2 tablespoons (30 ml) fresh dill
- 3 tablespoons (45 ml) chopped onion
- 1 teaspoon (5 ml) sugar
- ½ teaspoon (3 ml) salt
- A dash of pepper

1. Place the potatoes in a large pot and add enough cold water to cover. Bring to a boil and cook for 20–30 minutes, or until tender when pierced with a knife.
2. Remove the potatoes from the water and let cool. Cut the potatoes into medium-size (¹/₂-inch thick) slices.
3. In a small bowl, mix the vinegar, water, lemon juice, oil, dill, onion, sugar, salt, and pepper. Pour over the potatoes and let sit for several minutes before serving.

 Quick Pasta Salad

Makes 10 servings

Nutrition Per Serving

Calories	210
Fat	3 g
Protein	7 g
Carbohydrates	40 g
Cholesterol	1 mg
Sodium	153 mg

This recipe will make enough to serve a crowd. If you're cooking for just yourself, halve the ingredients and save the leftovers for quick lunches and snacks.

1 16-ounce (454 g) box tricolor pasta (we recommend fusilli)
1 cup (250 ml) chopped broccoli
2 carrots, peeled and chopped

1 onion, thinly sliced
1 red bell pepper, chopped
1 cucumber, peeled and sliced
¾ cup (185 ml) Italian dressing (see page 130 for our recipe)

1. Bring a large pot of water to a boil. Add the pasta and cook until tender, about 8 minutes. Drain.
2. While the pasta is cooking, place the broccoli, carrots, onion, and red pepper in a microwave-safe bowl. Cook in a microwave on high for 3 minutes. (If you don't have a microwave, blanch the vegetables.)
3. Combine the cooked vegetables and cucumber with the pasta. Cover and refrigerate until chilled.
4. Pour the dressing over the salad when ready to serve. Toss to coat.

Fruit Salad

Makes 4 servings

Nutrition Per Serving

Calories	97
Fat	Less than 1 g
Protein	4 g
Carbohydrates	21 g
Cholesterol	1 mg
Sodium	45 mg

A great summer and spring salad.

2 medium apples, peeled and chopped
1 tangerine, peeled and chopped
1 cup (250 ml) halved seedless green grapes

½ cup (125 ml) washed and sliced strawberries
1 tablespoon (15 ml) chopped fresh mint
1 cup (250 ml) nonfat plain yogurt

1. In a large bowl, combine all the ingredients and mix well.
2. For best flavor, refrigerate overnight.

Mandarin Orange and Mint Salad

Makes 4 servings

This makes a light and delicious salad that's great for the spring or summer months. When you serve it, make sure plenty of mint and orange go into each bowl.

Nutrition Per Serving	
Calories	56
Fat	Less than 1 g
Protein	3 g
Carbohydrates	12 g
Cholesterol	0 mg
Sodium	11 mg

1 head romaine lettuce, washed and [chopped]
1 tablespoon (15 ml) finely chopped fresh mint

3 whole mandarin oranges, peeled and separated

Combine all the ingredients and toss well.

Green Bean Salad

Makes 4 servings

A scrumptious way to get your vegetables, this salad works equally well with French, ranch, or vinaigrette dressing. You choose.

Nutrition Per Serving	
Calories	69
Fat	4 g
Protein	2 g
Carbohydrates	8 g
Cholesterol	0 mg
Sodium	53 mg

1 pound (450 g) fresh green beans
1/3 cup (80 ml) thinly sliced red onion

1/4 cup (60 ml) salad dressing of choice

1. Wash the green beans and snip off their ends.
2. Bring a large pot of water to a boil. Carefully drop in the green beans and blanch for 4 minutes. Drain and rinse in cold water.
3. Toss the onion with the beans and add salad dressing to taste.

# Coleslaw

Makes 4 servings

Perfect for picnics and cookouts.

Nutrition Per Serving

Calories	72
Fat	2 g
Protein	1 g
Carbohydrates	6 g
Cholesterol	1 mg
Sodium	139 mg

¼ head cabbage, shredded
1 carrot, shredded
½ cup (125 ml) finely chopped red onion
¼ cup (60 ml) low-fat vinaigrette dressing

2 tablespoons (30 ml) nonfat plain yogurt
1 tablespoon (15 ml) cider vinegar
Pepper to taste

Mix all the ingredients well. Refrigerate until ready to serve.

Egg Salad

Makes 1 serving

Serve on lettuce as a salad or in a pita pocket as a sandwich.

Nutrition Per Serving

Calories	69
Fat	4 g
Protein	6 g
Carbohydrates	1 g
Cholesterol	181 mg
Sodium	90 mg

1 hard-boiled egg
1½ teaspoons (8 ml) nonfat plain yogurt

½ teaspoon (3 ml) Dijon mustard
Salt and pepper to taste

1. Finely chop the egg.
2. In a small bowl, thoroughly mix the chopped egg with the yogurt and mustard. Season with salt and pepper.

★ Chicken Salad

Makes 4 servings

Serve over salad greens or as a sandwich filling.

2 cups (500 ml) cooked, chopped chicken

¼ cup (125 ml) nonfat plain yogurt

2 teaspoons (10 ml) mustard

3 tablespoons (45 ml) chopped celery

¼ cup (60 ml) chopped seedless green grapes

Salt and pepper to taste

Combine all the ingredients and stir until well mixed. Refrigerate or serve immediately.

Nutrition Per Serving	
Calories	167
Fat	6 g
Protein	22 g
Carbohydrates	4 g
Cholesterol	65 mg
Sodium	110 mg

⏱ Tuna Salad

Makes 2 servings

Serve on greens or in a sandwich — this salad is tasty either way. Makes great leftovers.

1 6-ounce (170 g) can white tuna in water, drained

2 tablespoons (30 ml) nonfat plain yogurt

½ teaspoon (3 ml) Dijon mustard

¼ of a medium carrot, grated

Salt and pepper to taste

Combine all the ingredients and stir well. Refrigerate or serve immediately.

Nutrition Per Serving	
Calories	110
Fat	Less than 1 g
Protein	23 g
Carbohydrates	2 g
Cholesterol	26 mg
Sodium	265 mg

Chapter 5

Vegetarian Delights

We have included a great variety of suggestions for vegetarian cooking in this section. However, vegetarian options are in no way confined to this section. There are many more vegetarian recipes throughout the book — just look for the . As for what "vegetarian" means, in this book vegetarian suggestions do not use eggs, fish, shellfish, or meat of any sort. Please note that many of our pastas are marked vegetarian. Although most pasta has egg in it, eggless brands are available.

Vegetable Chili

Makes 10 servings

This is a great winter dish. We recommend making this one for a large group of friends, or just making up a large batch over the weekend to freeze for quick meals throughout the week. Try serving it with warm corn bread, corn chips, or rice.

Nutrition Per Serving	
Calories	533
Fat	3 g
Protein	32 g
Carbohydrates	101 g
Cholesterol	0 mg
Sodium	252 mg

Nonstick cooking spray
1 yellow onion, diced
2 green peppers, diced
2 14.5 ounce (411 g) cans stewed whole tomatoes
2 15-ounce (425 g) cans black beans
1 16-ounce (456 g) can cooked corn
1 15-ounce (425 g) can kidney beans
½ tablespoon (8 ml) chili powder
1 teaspoon (5 ml) cayenne
½ teaspoon (3 ml) cinnamon
Salt and pepper to taste
2 fresh tomatoes, diced
2 cups (500 ml) shredded low-fat cheddar cheese (optional)

1. Spray a large pot with nonstick cooking spray. Over medium heat, sauté the onion and peppers until they just begin to brown.
2. Add all the canned ingredients, including the liquid from the cans, as well as the chili powder, cayenne, and cinnamon to the pot. Bring to a boil, reduce heat, and simmer for at least 30 minutes, or until the mixture reaches desired consistency. Season with salt and pepper.
3. Ladle into bowls, topping with diced tomatoes and cheddar cheese.

KITCHEN QUICK TIP

Vitamin C

Did you know that red and green bell peppers have more vitamin C than oranges do? Raw green bells have about twice as much, while red bells have four times as much!

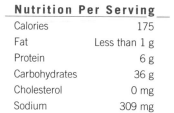

Teriyaki Couscous

Makes 4 servings

If you don't have all of the vegetables listed on hand, just use what you have.

Nutrition Per Serving

Calories	175
Fat	Less than 1 g
Protein	6 g
Carbohydrates	36 g
Cholesterol	0 mg
Sodium	309 mg

½ cup (125 ml) chopped onion
½ cup (125 ml) chopped green pepper
½ cup (125 ml) cleaned and chopped mushrooms
½ cup (125 ml) chopped eggplant

3 teaspoons (15 ml) minced ginger
2 tablespoons (30 ml) low-sodium soy sauce
1 teaspoon (5 ml) white vinegar
3 cups (750 ml) cooked couscous

1. In a large skillet over medium heat, sauté the vegetables and 2 teaspoons of the ginger in 1 tablespoon of the soy sauce. Cook to desired tenderness.
2. Add the vinegar, couscous, and remaining soy sauce and ginger. Cook for 1 minute over high heat, stirring often.

Curried Potatoes

Makes 4 servings

A favorite of a student at the Massachusetts Institute of Technology.

Nutrition Per Serving

Calories	183
Fat	5 g
Protein	4 g
Carbohydrates	31 g
Cholesterol	0 mg
Sodium	727 mg

1½ tablespoons (23 ml) extra-virgin olive oil
2 large potatoes, peeled and sliced
1 small onion, chopped
1 tablespoon (15 ml) curry powder

1 teaspoon (5 ml) minced ginger
½ teaspoon (3 ml) salt
1 teaspoon (5 ml) sugar
3 tablespoons (45 ml) low-sodium soy sauce

1. In a large pan, warm the oil over medium heat. Add the potatoes and cook, stirring often, for 15 minutes or until browned.
2. Add the onion, curry, and ginger to the pan. Mix and cook for 1 minute. Add the salt, sugar, and soy sauce. Cook for another 5 minutes and serve.

★ Eggplant Parmesan

Makes 6 servings

Great not only when fresh from the oven but also in a sandwich the next day.

½ cup (125 ml) bread crumbs
1 tablespoon (15 ml) dried oregano
1 tablespoon (15 ml) dried basil
1 medium eggplant, cut into ½-inch (3 cm) slices
5 tablespoons (75 ml) extra-virgin olive oil
1 clove garlic, minced

2½ cups (625 ml) crushed tomatoes
Salt and pepper to taste
⅓ of a 16-ounce (453 g) block of mozzarella cheese (or enough to cover the dish), thinly sliced
¼ cup (60 ml) grated Parmesan cheese

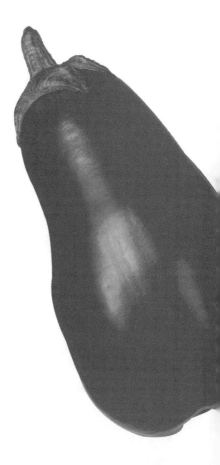

Nutrition Per Serving	
Calories	218
Fat	12 g
Protein	11 g
Carbohydrates	19 g
Cholesterol	4 mg
Sodium	536 mg

1. Preheat the oven to 350°F (180°C).
2. In a shallow dish, combine the bread crumbs, oregano, and basil.
3. Dip each slice of eggplant in the bread crumbs, coating both sides.
4. In a skillet over medium heat, cook the eggplant slices in just a touch of oil (save at least 1 teaspoon of oil for later use) for about 2 minutes a side, or until light brown.
5. Place the eggplant in a single layer in an ungreased baking dish.
6. In a saucepan over medium heat, warm the reserved teaspoon of oil. Sauté the garlic for 2 minutes, then add the tomatoes, salt, and pepper. Continue cooking until the mixture is thoroughly heated.
7. Pour the tomato mixture over the eggplant slices. Top with mozzarella and sprinkle Parmesan evenly over the dish.
8. Bake for 30 minutes. Remove from the oven and allow to cool for 10 minutes before serving.

KITCHEN QUICK TIP

The Truth about Eggplant

Did you know that eggplant is technically not a vegetable, but rather a berry? Also, eggplant is an excellent source of potassium.

Sesame Noodles

Makes 4 servings

This is an incredibly fast recipe, especially if you have leftover pasta in the fridge. We find it's best served cold.

Nutrition Per Serving

Calories	325
Fat	11 g
Protein	11 g
Carbohydrates	46 g
Cholesterol	0 mg
Sodium	81 mg

- ½ of a 16-ounce (454 g) package of spaghetti, cooked
- 4 tablespoons (60 ml) peanut butter
- 2 teaspoons (10 ml) sesame oil
- ½ teaspoon (3 ml) cider vinegar
- 1 tablespoon (15 ml) chopped scallions (optional)

1. Cook the peanut butter and sesame oil in a small bowl in the microwave for 30 seconds, or until the peanut butter begins to melt. Mix well. (If you don't have a microwave, you can also do this in a skillet over low heat.)
2. Blend the peanut butter mixture into the pasta. Add scallions. Refrigerate and serve cold.

★Caramelized Onion Orzo

Makes 4 servings

This is one of our favorites — it's very easy and delicious. Orzo is a small, delicate pasta that looks a lot like rice. You should be able to find it in the pasta section of your local supermarket.

Nutrition Per Serving

Calories	302
Fat	4 g
Protein	8 g
Carbohydrates	59 g
Cholesterol	8 mg
Sodium	39 mg

- 1 8-ounce (228 g) package orzo
- 1 tablespoon (15 ml) butter
- 3 tablespoons (45 ml) brown sugar, firmly packed
- 2 medium onions, chopped

1. Cook the orzo in 2 quarts (2 l) of boiling water until tender, about 8 minutes. Drain.
2. In a skillet over medium heat, melt the butter and brown sugar. Add the onions and sauté until brown.
3. In a serving dish, combine the onion mixture with the orzo. Serve warm.

Ginger-Soy Tofu with Rice

Makes 4 servings

From a friend at New York University in New York, New York.

1 tablespoon (15 ml) extra-virgin olive oil
1 1-pound (454 g) package firm tofu, drained, rinsed, and sliced
⅓ cup (80 ml) low-sodium soy sauce
1 teaspoon (5 ml) minced ginger
3 cups (750 ml) cooked white rice (about 1½ cups, or 375 ml, uncooked)

Nutrition Per Serving	
Calories	310
Fat	9 g
Protein	14 g
Carbohydrates	43 g
Cholesterol	0 mg
Sodium	811 mg

1. In a large skillet, warm the oil over medium heat. Add the tofu and sauté for 5 minutes.
2. In a small bowl, combine the soy sauce and ginger.
3. Add half of the soy sauce mixture to the skillet. Reduce heat to low and cook the tofu for 2 minutes.
4. Flip the strips of tofu and add the remaining half of the soy sauce mixture. Cook for 5 minutes.
5. Serve over hot cooked rice.

Black Beans and Onions

Makes 4 servings

This recipe takes practically no time. It's good on its own (hot or cold) or as a topping for brown rice. If you're planning on having this as your main dish, you might want to make a bit more than what is called for here.

1 teaspoon (5 ml) butter
1 15-ounce (425 g) can black beans
1 medium onion, chopped
Salt and pepper to taste

Nutrition Per Serving	
Calories	385
Fat	2 g
Protein	23 g
Carbohydrates	69 g
Cholesterol	3 mg
Sodium	16 mg

1. Melt the margarine in a skillet over medium heat. Add the onion and sauté for 5 minutes. The onion should stay crisp, not brown.
2. Add the beans and cook for 3–4 more minutes. Season with salt and pepper.

✿ ★ Garlic Green Beans with Tofu

Makes 4 servings

This recipe makes four servings as a side dish, two servings as a main dish.

1 pound (450 g) green beans
2 tablespoons (30 ml)
   vegetable oil
4 cloves garlic, minced

½ of a 1-pound (454 g) block
   of firm tofu, drained, rinsed,
   and cut into bite-size pieces
Salt and pepper to taste

1. Rinse the beans and snip off their ends.
2. In a wok or nonstick skillet, warm the oil over medium heat. Add the beans and garlic and sauté for 5 minutes, stirring continuously.
3. Add the tofu and cook for 5 more minutes.

✿ Red Beans and Rice

Makes 4 servings

Serve these spicy beans over hot cooked rice.

1 teaspoon (5 ml) butter
1 small yellow onion, chopped
½ green pepper, chopped
1 stalk celery, chopped
2 15-ounce (425 g) cans
   kidney beans, drained
   and rinsed

2 cloves garlic, minced
½ teaspoon (3 ml) dried oregano
½ cup (125 ml) tomato sauce
1 tablespoon (15 ml) hot sauce
2 tablespoons (30 ml)
   Worcestershire sauce
Salt and pepper to taste

1. In a large skillet melt the butter over medium heat. Add the onion and sauté until it becomes translucent.
2. Add the pepper, celery, beans, garlic, oregano, tomato sauce, hot sauce, and Worcestershire. Simmer over a low heat for 10 minutes. Season with salt and pepper and serve immediately.

★Anna's Veggie Lasagna

Makes 8 servings

This one is highly recommended for large groups or potlucks. Enjoy.

- 1 16-ounce (454 g) package lasagna noodles
- ½ tablespoon (8 ml) extra-virgin olive oil
- 1 large yellow onion, chopped
- 2 carrots, grated
- 1 medium zucchini, chopped
- 1½ cups chopped white mushrooms
- 3 lightly packed cups (750 ml) fresh, washed spinach
- 1 16-ounce (454 g) tub non-fat cottage cheese
- Salt and pepper to taste
- 5 cups (1.25 l) tomato sauce
- 1½ cups (375 ml) shredded low-fat mozzarella cheese

Nutrition Per Serving	
Calories	381
Fat	6 g
Protein	24 g
Carbohydrates	60 g
Cholesterol	14 mg
Sodium	1,212 mg

1. Preheat the oven to 350°F (180°C).
2. Bring a large pot of water to a boil. Add the noodles and cook until noodles are pliable but only half cooked, about 4–5 minutes. Remove from heat and place the noodles in a bowl of cold water to stop the cooking.
3. Heat the oil in a large skillet over medium heat. Sauté the onion, carrots, and zucchini until the onion becomes translucent, about 3 minutes. Add the mushrooms and continue to sauté until they begin to soften, about 3 minutes. Add the spinach and cook about 3 more minutes, until it wilts and shrinks.
4. Add the cottage cheese and cook for 5–7 minutes, until the flavors are well mixed. Season with salt and pepper. Remove from heat and drain any excess liquid from the pan.
5. Spread a thin layer of tomato sauce in a large lasagna pan. Place a layer of noodles on top of it, followed by a layer of cheese and then a layer of the sautéed vegetables. Repeat until the dish is almost full. Top with a layer of noodles covered with a layer of cheese. Cover with aluminum foil and bake for 40 minutes.

Tofu and Broccoli Stir-Fry

Makes 2 servings

This recipe includes a great peanut sauce, but if you're not one for peanut butter, don't skip over the whole recipe — try a splash of soy sauce instead. Both variations are great over brown or white rice.

1 tablespoon (15 ml) peanut butter	2 teaspoons (10 ml) sesame or canola oil
1 tablespoon (15 ml) hot water	3 cups (750 ml) chopped broccoli
1 tablespoon (15 ml) cider vinegar	2 cloves garlic, minced
1 tablespoon (15 ml) low-sodium soy sauce	½ of a 1-pound (454 g) block of firm tofu, cut into small cubes

1. In a small bowl, stir together the peanut butter, hot water, vinegar, and soy sauce. If it is difficult to mix, heat it in the microwave for 10 seconds.
2. Warm the oil in a wok or large nonstick skillet over high heat. Add the broccoli and garlic and cook for 5 minutes, stirring constantly.
3. Add in the tofu, and cook for an additional 5 minutes. Remove from heat.
4. Mix in the sauce until the tofu and broccoli are well coated.

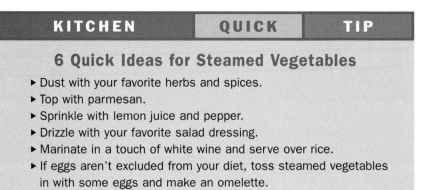

KITCHEN QUICK TIP

6 Quick Ideas for Steamed Vegetables

▶ Dust with your favorite herbs and spices.
▶ Top with parmesan.
▶ Sprinkle with lemon juice and pepper.
▶ Drizzle with your favorite salad dressing.
▶ Marinate in a touch of white wine and serve over rice.
▶ If eggs aren't excluded from your diet, toss steamed vegetables in with some eggs and make an omelette.

Chapter 6

Lots of Pasta

Pasta seems to have acquired a reputation as a last-resort lifesaver for most college students cooking on their own. While spaghetti with tomato sauce and microwave macaroni and cheese are certainly worthwhile dishes for any first-time cook, we hope to provide you with a somewhat more extensive range of pasta options.

We've listed some great pasta sauces in this chapter. However, to figure out the nutritional information of a serving of sauce over a serving-size portion of pasta (usually 2 ounces, or 56 g), you'll need to know the nutritional breakdown for plain pasta. Here's a comparison of 2 ounces of enriched pasta versus 2 ounces of whole wheat pasta:

Enriched Pasta		Whole Wheat Pasta	
Calories	210	Calories	220
Fat	1 g	Fat	3 g
Carbohydrates	42 g	Carbohydrates	43 g
Protein	7 g	Protein	7 g
Cholesterol	0 g	Cholesterol	0 g
Sodium	7 g	Sodium	1 g

★Basic Tomato Sauce

Makes 4 servings

Nutrition Per Serving

Calories	79
Fat	2 g
Protein	3 g
Carbohydrates	16 g
Cholesterol	0 mg
Sodium	1,082 mg

This recipe is far better than the ready-made stuff and will save you money in the long run. For a little variety, you can add almost any vegetable from your refrigerator. You can serve it over any pasta in your cupboard — we prefer spaghetti.

1 teaspoon (5 ml) extra-virgin olive oil	¼ teaspoon (1 ml) salt
2 cloves garlic, minced	¼ teaspoon (1 ml) freshly ground pepper
1 20-ounce (570 g) can tomato sauce	1 teaspoon (5 ml) dried basil
1 6-ounce (170 g) can tomato paste	1 teaspoon (5 ml) dried oregano

1. In a saucepan, warm the oil over medium heat. Add the garlic and sauté for about 1 minute, until garlic is slightly browned.
2. Add the tomato sauce and paste, salt, pepper, basil, and oregano, and mix well. Bring to a boil, then reduce heat and simmer for 5 minutes.
3. Serve immediately over hot pasta, or cool and ladle into containers for refrigeration or freezing.

KITCHEN QUICK TIP

For a Little Variety

To make your tomato sauce a little more exciting, we recommend sautéing vegetables along with the garlic before adding the tomato sauce. If you want to add meat, make sure it's cooked well before adding it to your sauce. Here are some suggestions for additions to your sauce:

- ▸ Zucchini and yellow squash
- ▸ Mushrooms
- ▸ Spinach
- ▸ Onion
- ▸ Broccoli
- ▸ Ground beef

Tomato-Basil Sauce

Makes 4 servings

This is a great simple sauce that's good over all kinds of pasta.

1 teaspoon (5 ml) extra-virgin olive oil
2 cloves garlic, minced
Salt and pepper to taste

½ of a 28-ounce (793 g) can crushed tomatoes, drained (the rest can be frozen for the next time you need them)
1 tablespoon (15 ml) chopped fresh basil

Nutrition Per Serving	
Calories	37
Fat	1 g
Protein	1 g
Carbohydrates	7 g
Cholesterol	0 mg
Sodium	252 mg

1. Warm the oil in a saucepan over medium heat. Add the garlic and sauté, stirring continuously, for about 2 minutes, or until slightly browned. Season with salt and pepper.
2. Add the tomatoes and cook for 10 minutes, stirring often.
3. Add the basil and stir well. Pour over hot pasta and serve immediately.

★Spinach-Ricotta Sauce

Makes 4 servings

We recommend serving this over fresh-cooked penne.

2 teaspoons (10 ml) extra-virgin olive oil
1 medium onion, chopped
2 cloves garlic, minced
1 cup (250 ml) cooked spinach
1 cup (250 ml) nonfat ricotta cheese

1 large tomato, chopped
¼ teaspoon (1 ml) freshly ground pepper
Salt to taste
¼ cup (60 ml) grated Parmesan cheese

Nutrition Per Serving	
Calories	120
Fat	4 g
Protein	13 g
Carbohydrates	10 g
Cholesterol	280 mg
Sodium	183 mg

1. In a large skillet, warm the oil over medium heat. Add the onion and garlic and sauté until the onion becomes translucent.
2. Add the spinach, ricotta, tomato, and pepper. Mix thoroughly; season with salt.
3. Add the Parmesan; mix well. Pour over hot pasta.

Sweet Red Pepper Sauce

Makes 4 servings

A sweeter variation of the usual tomato-based sauce.

1 teaspoon (5 ml) extra-virgin olive oil
2 red bell peppers, chopped
2 carrots, chopped
2 medium tomatoes, chopped
1 clove garlic, minced
1 pear, sliced
1 teaspoon (5 ml) salt
½ teaspoon (3 ml) black pepper
1 teaspoon (5 ml) dried basil

1. In a skillet, warm the oil over medium heat. Add the peppers and carrots and sauté until soft, about 10 minutes.
2. Add to the skillet the tomatoes, garlic, pear, salt, pepper, and basil. Reduce heat and cook until soft, about 30 minutes.
3. Puree the sautéed mixture in a blender. Serve over hot pasta.

Shrimp and Feta Pasta

Makes 4 servings

This recipe makes a great meal for guests and dates.

2 teaspoons (10 ml) extra-virgin olive oil
3 cloves garlic, minced
1 cup (250 ml) chopped onion
2 cups (500 ml) tomato sauce
1 medium tomato, chopped
Oregano to taste
Basil to taste
½ cup (125 ml) white wine
1 pound (450 g) raw shrimp, shelled and deveined
½ of a 16-ounce (454 g) package spaghetti or linguine, cooked
½ cup (125 ml) crumbled feta cheese

1. In a large skillet, warm the oil over medium heat. Add the garlic and onion and sauté until the onion is translucent. Add the tomato sauce and tomatoes and cook until warmed through.
2. Add the white wine to the skillet and heat until the mixture is bubbling. Then add the shrimp and cook until pink.
3. Spoon the sauce over hot pasta and top with crumbled feta cheese.

Emily's Pasta Sauce

Makes 4 servings

Serve this recipe over hot bow tie pasta. It's also delicious if you cook the mushrooms in $1/3$ cup sherry.

Nutrition Per Serving	
Calories	30
Fat	2 g
Protein	2 g
Carbohydrates	2 g
Cholesterol	5 mg
Sodium	69 mg

1 teaspoon (5 ml) butter or margarine
1½ cups (375 ml) sliced mushrooms

1 clove garlic, minced
A pinch of salt
2 tablespoons (30 ml) grated Parmesan cheese

1. In a skillet, melt the butter over medium heat. Add the mushrooms and garlic and sauté until the mushrooms are soft, about 8 minutes. Add the salt.
2. Spoon the mushrooms over hot pasta and sprinkle with Parmesan cheese.

Macaroni and Cheese

Makes 4 servings

A healthy alternative to the boxed variety.

Nutrition Per Serving	
Calories	276
Fat	8 g
Protein	15 g
Carbohydrates	36 g
Cholesterol	25 mg
Sodium	196 mg

1¾ cups (435 ml) uncooked macaroni
1 cup (250 ml) shredded low-fat cheddar cheese
¼ cup (60 ml) nonfat plain yogurt

2 teaspoons (10 ml) butter
½ tablespoon (8 ml) Dijon mustard
Salt and pepper to taste

1. Bring a large pot of water to a boil. Add the macaroni and cook until tender, about 8 minutes.
2. While the pasta is cooking, mix together the cheese and yogurt in a bowl.
3. When the pasta is done, drain and set aside. Put the pot back on the stove and melt the butter over medium heat. Stir in the mustard, salt, and pepper. Add the cooked macaroni, tossing to coat. Mix in the cheese and yogurt. Continue to cook, stirring constantly, until the cheese is melted.

★Fancy Asparagus Pasta

Makes 4 servings

If you're hoping to impress, this is the dish to make.

½ of a 16-ounce (454 g) package penne pasta
14 asparagus stalks, cut to 1½-inch (4 cm) lengths
2 teaspoons (10 ml) extra-virgin olive oil
⅔ cup (160 ml) finely chopped onion
10 mushrooms, quartered
1 cup (250 ml) sliced cooked ham, cut to approximately the same width and length of asparagus
1 cup (250 ml) light cream
Salt and pepper to taste

1. Bring a large pot of water to a boil. Add the pasta and cook until tender, about 10 minutes. Drain; set aside.
2. Place the asparagus in a pot and fill with ¼- to ½-inch of water. Bring to a boil, reduce heat, and steam the asparagus until tender, about 7–10 minutes.
3. In a large skillet, warm the oil over medium heat. Add the onion and sauté until it begins to turn translucent. Add the mushrooms and ham, and cook until mushrooms are drained of liquid.
4. Add the asparagus to the skillet and pour in the cream. Continue to cook over low heat until the sauce thickens, about 8 minutes. Pour the sauce over the drained pasta and mix well. Serve immediately.

Ramen Noodle Stir-Fry

Makes 2 servings

Many brands of instant noodles are high in fat, so be sure to buy the lowfat variety.

1 package baked ramen noodles (any flavor — you won't use the seasoning)
1 teaspoon (5 ml) extra-virgin olive oil
¼ cup (60 ml) chopped green pepper
¼ cup (60 ml) chopped red bell pepper
¼ cup (60 ml) chopped onion
1 clove garlic, minced
1 teaspoon (5 ml) hot sauce
Oregano to taste
Cayenne to taste

Nutrition Per Serving	
Calories	128
Fat	2 g
Protein	5 g
Carbohydrates	24 g
Cholesterol	0 mg
Sodium	227 mg

1. Bring a pot of water to a boil. Add the noodles and cook until tender, about 3 minutes.
2. Warm the oil in a large skillet over medium heat. Add the peppers, onion, and garlic and sauté until the vegetables are tender. Add the hot sauce, oregano, and cayenne, and let simmer for 5 minutes.
3. Add the noodles to the skillet and cook for about 1 minute, or until thoroughly mixed and heated.

Mushroom Pasta Sauce

Makes 3 servings

For anyone who's a fan of mushrooms, this is the sauce for you.

3 tablespoons (45 ml) butter
3 cups (750 ml) sliced mushrooms
⅓ cup (80 ml) white wine
1½ tablespoons (23 ml) flour
1¼ cups (310 ml) 2% milk
¼ teaspoon (3 ml) salt
¼ teaspoon (1 ml) pepper

Nutrition Per Serving	
Calories	200
Fat	14 g
Protein	5 g
Carbohydrates	11 g
Cholesterol	38 mg
Sodium	348 mg

1. In a large skillet, melt the butter over medium heat. Add the mushrooms and sauté until they become soft and begin producing their own juice. Add the wine, turn up the heat to high, and cook until the wine has been absorbed.
2. Turn heat to low. Add the flour, coating the mushrooms. Slowly add the milk and stir until the sauce thickens. Season with salt and pepper. Pour over hot pasta.

★Pesto Pasta with Sun-Dried Tomatoes

Makes 4 servings

This recipe comes compliments of a student at Georgetown University.

Nutrition Per Serving	
Calories	410
Fat	19 g
Protein	14 g
Carbohydrates	47 g
Cholesterol	10 mg
Sodium	381 mg

½ of a 16-ounce (454 g) package pasta
¼ cup (60 ml) extra-virgin olive oil
1 tablespoon (15 ml) water
2 cups (500 ml) fresh basil leaves

1 clove garlic, chopped
¼ cup (60 ml) pine nuts
½ cup (125 ml) grated Parmesan cheese
½ cup (125 ml) thinly sliced sun-dried tomatoes

1. Bring a large pot of water to a boil. Add the pasta and cook until tender, about 8–10 minutes. Drain.
2. While the pasta is cooking, combine the oil, water, basil, garlic, pine nuts, and ¹/₄ cup of the Parmesan cheese in a blender and puree.
3. Toss the pesto with the pasta, tomatoes, and remaining cheese. Serve hot.

Teriyaki Salmon over Pasta

Makes 4 servings

We recommend serving this over wide noodles.

Nutrition Per Serving	
Calories	302
Fat	5 g
Protein	18 g
Carbohydrates	44 g
Cholesterol	29 mg
Sodium	300 mg

1 teaspoon (5 ml) extra-virgin olive oil
6 medium mushrooms, sliced
1 clove garlic, minced
Low-sodium soy sauce to taste

Minced ginger to taste
1 7.5-ounce (213 g) can pink salmon, drained
½ of a 16-ounce (454 g) package pasta, cooked

1. In a large skillet, warm the oil over medium heat. Add the mushrooms and garlic and sauté until the mushrooms begin to soften. Add the soy sauce and ginger. Mix well. Raise heat to medium-high and cook for 3 more minutes.
2. Mix in the salmon, adding more soy sauce to taste. Add the cooked pasta and stir well. Cook for 2 more minutes, stirring constantly. Serve hot.

★ Baked Ziti

Makes 4 servings

For a vegetarian alternative, omit the beef and add your favorite vegetable.

½ of a 16-ounce (454 g)
  package ziti
½ pound (225 g) lean
  ground beef
½ yellow onion, finely chopped
2 cloves garlic, minced

2 cups (500 ml) tomato sauce
Oregano to taste
Basil to taste
Salt to taste
1 cup (250 ml) shredded
  mozzarella cheese

Nutrition Per Serving	
Calories	386
Fat	11 g
Protein	20 g
Carbohydrates	53 g
Cholesterol	39 mg
Sodium	783 mg

1. Preheat the oven to 350°F (180°C).
2. Bring a large pot of water to a boil. Add the ziti and cook for about 8 minutes. The ziti should be slightly undercooked and chewy. Drain; set aside.
3. In a large skillet over medium heat, brown the beef with onion and garlic. Stir in the tomato sauce, herbs, and salt.
4. Mix the ziti with the sauce and cheese in an ovenproof dish, saving some cheese to sprinkle on top. Cover with aluminum foil and bake for 20 minutes.

 Lazy Pasta

Makes 4 servings

This recipe comes from a friend at Colorado College in Colorado Springs.

½ of a 16-ounce (454 g)
  package pasta
3 teaspoons (15 ml) butter
1 small zucchini, sliced
6 mushrooms, quartered

1 tomato, diced
¼ cup (60 ml) grated
  Parmesan cheese
1½ teaspoons (8 ml) skim milk

Nutrition Per Serving	
Calories	276
Fat	6 g
Protein	11 g
Carbohydrates	45 g
Cholesterol	13 mg
Sodium	153 mg

1. Bring a large pot of water to a boil. Add the pasta, cook until desired tenderness, and drain.
2. While the pasta is cooking, melt 2 teaspoons of the butter in a large skillet over medium heat. Add the zucchini and mushrooms and sauté until soft. Add the tomato and cook for 1 more minute.
3. Melt the remaining teaspoon of butter in the hot pasta. Add the cheese, milk, and vegetables. Stir well and serve.

Orzo with Ham and Vegetables

Makes 4 servings

This quick pasta dish is delicious hot or cold.

1¼ cups (310 ml) uncooked orzo
1 teaspoon (5 ml) extra-virgin olive oil
1 cup (250 ml) diced cooked ham
⅓ cup (80 ml) finely chopped onion
⅓ cup (80 ml) corn kernels (fresh or frozen)
⅓ cup (80 ml) green beans, chopped into ½-inch (1 cm) lengths
3 tablespoons (45 ml) Dijon mustard
2 tablespoons (30 ml) nonfat plain yogurt
2 tablespoons (30 ml) red wine vinegar

1. Bring a large pot of water to a boil. Add the orzo and cook until tender, about 8 minutes. Drain; set aside.
2. In a large skillet, warm 1 teaspoon oil over medium heat. Add the onion and sauté for 5 minutes. Add the ham and cook for an additional 3 minutes, then add the corn and green beans. Continue to cook until heated through.
3. In a large bowl, combine the ham, vegetables, and orzo, and mix well. Stir in the mustard, yogurt, and vinegar, and mix thoroughly.

Chapter 7

The Best of Seafood

Although it's true that there are some people who just plain don't like fish, we find the idea incredibly hard to believe. The usual complaint is, "Fish is just too fishy." Not true! While some varieties have a stronger fish flavor than others, fish is, for the most part, light and healthy with a nonintrusive flavor. We suggest you give it a chance. Compared to beef, pork, and chicken (and especially when you take into account hefty bones and the extra fat that has to be trimmed off for those cuts of meat), many kinds of fish are relatively inexpensive — you'll do best to browse the fresh seafood section of the market — as well as quick to prepare and easy to clean up. To make life a lot simpler, we have included a number of great oven and microwave tips for poaching fish.

When buying fish, always make sure that it's fresh. Don't buy fish that is discolored in any way. Check the expiration date and smell the fish before cooking (this is good advice for any type of meat). Fish can be frozen prior to use, and should be eaten soon after cooking.

Brett's Versatile Fish Steak

Makes 4 servings

If you have a barbecue grill and are in the mood, you can grill this fish steak over fire.

1½ pounds (675 g) fish steak (we recommend tuna)	1 cup (250 ml) vinaigrette of choice

1. Marinate the steak in the vinaigrette for two hours in the refrigerator.
2. Grill the fish for about 5 minutes per side, checking often, until the steak is done to your satisfaction (some people prefer tuna to stay slightly pink on the inside).

Light Lime Garlic Shrimp

Makes 4 servings

As most seafood lovers know, lime and shrimp are natural partners. The addition of garlic and a drop of hot sauce help spice up the dish.

Juice of one lime	½ teaspoon (3 ml) salt
2 cloves garlic, thickly sliced	1½–2 pounds (675 to 900 g)
1 tablespoon (15 ml) hot sauce	shrimp, peeled and deveined

1. Preheat the oven to 350°F (180°C).
2. In a small bowl, combine the lime juice, garlic, hot sauce, and salt.
3. Line a casserole dish with aluminum foil so that there is enough extra at each end to fold back over the dish. Place the shrimp in the dish, then pour the lime juice mixture in. Cover and bake for 7 minutes.

★ Festive Flounder

Makes 4 servings

A great recipe for entertaining.

¼ cup (60 ml) all-purpose flour
½ teaspoon (3 ml) pepper
4 6-ounce (170 g) flounder
   fillets
1 tablespoon (15 ml) extra-
   virgin olive oil

1 tablespoon (15 ml) butter
10 mushrooms, sliced
3 scallions, sliced
2 cloves garlic, minced
1 lemon, cut in half

Nutrition Per Serving	
Calories	251
Fat	5 g
Protein	17 g
Carbohydrates	13 g
Cholesterol	8 mg
Sodium	90 mg

1. Combine the flour and pepper on a large plate.
2. Pat the fish fillets dry with paper towels. Coat each fillet thoroughly with the flour mixture.
3. In a large skillet, warm the oil over medium-high heat. Cook the fillets (two at a time, if possible) for 2 minutes per side, flipping only once.
4. In a skillet, melt the butter over medium heat. Add the mushrooms, scallions, and garlic. Turn heat to high after a minute or two and stir often. Once the vegetables are cooked to your satisfaction, add the juice of one lemon half to the pan, then remove from heat.
5. Pour the vegetable mixture evenly over the fillets. Slice the remaining lemon half into four wedges and serve one with each fillet.

KITCHEN
QUICK **TIP**

Quick Cleanup

When broiling fish, place it on aluminum foil instead of directly on the broiler rack to minimize cleaning.

★ Tuna with Tomato, Onion, and Parsley Salsa

Makes 4 servings

A simple yet classy dish.

Nutrition Per Serving

Calories	265
Fat	8 g
Protein	41 g
Carbohydrates	5 g
Cholesterol	65 mg
Sodium	343 mg

4 large tomatoes, peeled, seeded, and finely chopped
1 small red onion, finely chopped
1 clove garlic, minced
2 tablespoons (30 ml) chopped fresh parsley
½ teaspoon (3 ml) salt
1 tablespoon (15 ml) red wine vinegar
4 tuna steaks

1. In a large bowl, combine all of the ingredients except the tuna and mix well. Chill.
2. Preheat the broiler. Place the tuna in a baking dish. Broil to desired doneness, about 5 to 8 minutes per side. Serve with a scoop of the chilled salsa.

Red Snapper and Capers

Makes 4 servings

Capers help put the snap in snapper.

Nutrition Per Serving

Calories	178
Fat	2 g
Protein	35 g
Carbohydrates	2 g
Cholesterol	63 mg
Sodium	213 mg

Juice of 1 lemon
2 teaspoons (10 ml) grated lemon rind
1 tablespoon (15 ml) water
4 cloves garlic, minced
⅓ cup (80 ml) small capers
A pinch of salt
A pinch of pepper
1½ pounds (675 g) red snapper fillets

1. Preheat the oven to 425°F (220°C).
2. In a mixing bowl, combine all the ingredients except the red snapper.
3. Place the red snapper fillets in a glass baking dish and pour the juice mixture over them. Bake for 7–10 minutes (cooking time will depend on the thickness of the fillets), until the fillets are flaky and of a uniform texture throughout.

⏱ Quick Cod

Makes 4 servings

The quickest fish dish you'll ever enjoy!

1½ pounds (675 g) cod, cut
   into 4 portions
   Lemon juice to taste

Pepper to taste
4 wedges lemon

1. Arrange the cod in a microwave-safe glass dish. Sprinkle with lemon juice and pepper.
2. Cover and microwave on high for 2–3 minutes. Check progress after 2 minutes. If the fish is almost done, cover and let sit for a minute, rather than microwaving for another minute. Serve with lemon wedges.

Nutrition Per Serving	
Calories	140
Fat	1 g
Protein	30 g
Carbohydrates	0 g
Cholesterol	73 mg
Sodium	92 mg

★ Sole with Orange Sauce

Makes 4 servings

Orange sauce is usually reserved for red meat and poultry, but matched with sole in this recipe, it makes a great-tasting meal.

½ tablespoon (8 ml) butter
½ tablespoon (8 ml) all-
   purpose flour
¾ cup (185 ml) orange juice

½ teaspoon (3 ml) grated
   orange rind
1½ pounds (675 g) sole fillets
1 lemon, cut into 6 wedges

1. In a saucepan, melt the butter over medium heat. Stir in the flour and cook for 1 minute. Add the orange juice and rind and cook, stirring often, until thickened. Turn the heat to high and cook for 1–2 more minutes to thicken the sauce.
2. Place the fillets in a microwave-safe dish (you may need to do this in several batches) and squeeze the juice from two lemon wedges over them.
3. Cover the dish and cook on high in the microwave for 2 minutes. After the first minute, check the fish every 30 seconds, as the amount of cooking time will depend on the thickness of the fillets and how many you put in the microwave at a time. When the center of the fillets becomes opaque, it's done.
4. Pour orange sauce over the fillets and serve with lemon wedges.

Nutrition Per Serving	
Calories	153
Fat	2 g
Protein	26 g
Carbohydrates	6 g
Cholesterol	4 mg
Sodium	110 mg

Scallops over a Bed of Rice

Makes 4 servings

For a spicy meal, be generous with the red pepper.

½ teaspoon (3 ml) extra-virgin olive oil
2 cloves garlic, minced
1 teaspoon (5 ml) minced ginger
A pinch of red pepper flakes or cayenne
1½ pounds (675 g) small scallops

½ cup (125 ml) water
3 tablespoons (45 ml) chopped fresh parsley
Salt and pepper to taste
4 cups (1 l) cooked white rice

1. In a large wok or skillet, warm the oil over medium heat. Sauté the garlic, ginger, and red pepper. After 20 seconds, add the water and the scallops. Cook until the scallops are opaque.
2. Remove from heat and stir in the parsley, salt, and pepper. Serve over hot rice.

★ Honey Dijon Salmon

Makes 4 servings

This is a great dish that doesn't require much work on your end.

2 tablespoons (30 ml) Dijon mustard
4 teaspoons (20 ml) honey
2 teaspoons (10 ml) chopped fresh parsley

¼ cup (60 ml) bread crumbs
4 salmon fillets, each 4–6 ounces (115 to 170 g)
4 lemon wedges

1. Preheat the oven to 450°F (230°C).
2. In a small bowl, mix the mustard and honey.
3. In a separate bowl, combine the bread crumbs and parsley.
4. Place the salmon in an ovenproof pan. Spoon the mustard mixture evenly over each fillet and sprinkle bread crumbs on top. Bake 10 minutes for each inch of thickness, or until the fish is flaky. Serve with lemon wedges.

★Turbot with Tomato-Mango Salsa

Makes 4 servings

Another classy-looking dish good for company.

½ mango, peeled and chopped
1½ medium tomatoes, seeded and chopped
½ onion, diced
1 teaspoon (5 ml) chopped parsley

1 teaspoon (5 ml) lemon juice
A pinch of pepper
4 6-ounce (170 g) turbot fillets

Nutrition Per Serving	
Calories	182
Fat	5 g
Protein	28 g
Carbohydrates	5 g
Cholesterol	82 mg
Sodium	257 mg

1. In a medium bowl, mix the mango, tomato, onion, parsley, and lemon juice. Cover and refrigerate until chilled.
2. Place the fillets in a microwave-safe dish. Cover and microwave on high for 2 minutes, and then check. The fish should be cooked through and have a flaky texture. (Depending on the size of the fillets, you may need to microwave them for another minute or two.)
3. Arrange the fillets on plates. Ladle some of the chilled salsa on top of each fillet and serve immediately.

Mom's Tips

Don't Let It Hang Around!

Fresh or defrosted fish should be kept in the coldest area of your refrigerator. Cook within 1 or 2 days.

Breaded Whitefish

Makes 4 servings

As easy to prepare as frozen fishsticks, but so much better.

1½ pounds (675 g) whitefish
¼ cup (60 ml) flour
1 tablespoon (15 ml) water
1 egg
1 cup (250 ml) bread crumbs
1 teaspoon (5 ml) dried sage

1 teaspoon (5 ml) dried thyme
1 teaspoon (5 ml) freshly ground pepper
½ teaspoon (3 ml) salt
½ teaspoon (3 ml) cayenne

1. Preheat the oven to 350°F (180°C).
2. Rinse the fish, pat dry, and coat with flour.
3. Beat together the egg and water. Thoroughly coat the fish with the egg mixture.
4. Combine the remaining ingredients and pat the mixture on the fish, completely covering it.
5. Place the fish on a rack in a baking pan. Bake for about 25 minutes (time varies depending on the thickness of the fish), until it's cooked through.

Chapter 8

Simple Chicken Dinners

In writing this book, our friends and families presented us with an astounding number of amazingly delicious chicken recipes. Chicken is perfect for lunch or dinner, and leftovers can be used in a variety of dishes. Most of our recipes call for boneless, skinless chicken breasts, as these are the healthiest and are easy to prepare, but thighs and legs can be substituted, and they cost less. Preparation usually involves no more than chopping up a few ingredients, throwing them in a pan with the chicken, and adding an easy sauce. The most time-consuming part of the process is the actual cooking time. Please note, what most of us consider to be a chicken breast is actually a half-breast; chicken breasts are made up of two pieces. Just to be clear, we've called for half-breasts in our recipes.

As with all raw meat, chicken can carry dangerous bacteria. However, you'll be fine as long as you are conscientious about rinsing raw chicken in cold water before cooking (pat it dry afterward) and cleaning your utensils, preparation area, and hands with hot suds after handling raw chicken.

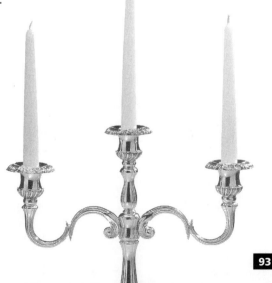

★ Sweet Orange Chicken

Makes 4 servings

This one gets five stars. Great hot or cold — though it's usually all gone before it has a chance to cool off.

Nutrition Per Serving

Calories	204
Fat	4 g
Protein	27 g
Carbohydrates	15 g
Cholesterol	70 mg
Sodium	159 mg

- **4 boneless, skinless chicken half-breasts**
- **4 teaspoons (20 ml) Dijon mustard**
- **½ medium onion, diced**
- **1 cup (250 ml) orange juice**
- **2 teaspoons (10 ml) butter**
- **2 tablespoons (30 ml) brown sugar**

1. Preheat the oven to 350°F (180°C).
2. Place the chicken in an ovenproof dish and spread mustard evenly over each piece. Sprinkle the onion over the chicken, pour orange juice over all, and place ½ teaspoon morsels of butter near each piece of chicken. Bake uncovered for 25 minutes.
3. Flip the chicken and sprinkle brown sugar evenly over each piece. Cook for an additional 10 minutes uncovered, or until cooked through (no pink shows in the middle).

Lemon Chicken

Makes 4 servings

Compliments of a student at the University of Pennsylvania.

Nutrition Per Serving

Calories	136
Fat	2 g
Protein	26 g
Carbohydrates	5 g
Cholesterol	65 mg
Sodium	74 mg

- **4 cloves garlic, minced**
- **¼ cup (60 ml) lemon juice**
- **½ teaspoon (3 ml) black pepper**
- **4 boneless, skinless chicken half-breasts**
- **4 lemon slices**

1. Preheat the oven to 350°F (180°C).
2. Combine the garlic, lemon juice, and pepper in a casserole dish. Add the chicken breasts and spoon some of the juice over each. Place one lemon slice on top of each chicken breast. Bake for 30 minutes, or until cooked through (no pink shows in the middle).

Apple Chicken

Makes 4 servings

Apple and mushrooms may seem like an odd combination, but give it a try. College is all about new experiences.

Nutrition Per Serving	
Calories	210
Fat	5 g
Protein	27 g
Carbohydrates	14 g
Cholesterol	65 mg
Sodium	210 mg

4 boneless, skinless chicken half-breasts
1 tablespoon (15 ml) extra-virgin olive oil
1 cup (250 ml) applesauce (see page 119 for our recipe)

8 medium mushrooms, sliced
¼ teaspoon (1 ml) salt, plus some to taste
Pepper to taste

1. Preheat the oven to 350°F (180°C).
2. In a large skillet, warm the oil over medium heat. Add the chicken breasts, and brown lightly on both sides.
3. Place the browned chicken in a casserole dish and cover evenly with apple-sauce. Sprinkle with ¼ teaspoon salt, cover, and bake for 25 minutes.
4. Add the mushrooms. Cover and bake for an additional 10 minutes. Season with salt and pepper.

Mom's Tips

Making Do

If your casserole dish doesn't have a cover, use aluminum foil instead.

★ Chicken with Green Peppers

Makes 4 servings

Nutrition Per Serving

Calories	144
Fat	2 g
Protein	27 g
Carbohydrates	4 g
Cholesterol	65 mg
Sodium	873 mg

While this is good hot, it's even better cold. Make lots to keep in the refrigerator as leftovers.

- 4 boneless, skinless chicken half-breasts
- 2 green peppers, chopped
- ⅓ cup (80 ml) low-sodium soy sauce

1. Preheat the oven to 350°F (180°C).
2. Arrange the chicken and peppers in an ovenproof pan large enough to accommodate all of them. Pour soy sauce over all.
3. Cover and bake for 30 minutes, or until cooked through (no pink shows in the middle).

Honey-Mustard and Garlic Chicken

Makes 4 servings

Nutrition Per Serving

Calories	211
Fat	3 g
Protein	27 g
Carbohydrates	20 g
Cholesterol	65 mg
Sodium	449 mg

Try serving this with a big green salad on the side.

- ¼ cup (60 ml) honey
- ½ cup (125 ml) Dijon mustard
- 4 boneless, skinless chicken half-breasts
- 1 clove garlic, cut into slivers

1. Preheat the oven to 350°F (180°C).
2. In a small bowl, combine the honey and mustard.
3. Make four small cuts in the center of each chicken breast, then arrange them in a baking dish. Insert a sliver of garlic into each cut. Spread the honey-mustard mixture over each breast.
4. Bake for 30 minutes, basting the chicken once or twice with sauce from the pan. Then transfer to the preheated broiler (or turn the oven temperature up to broil) and cook for 5 minutes, until the tops are crisp (but not burnt).

★Chicken Pesto Pasta

Makes 5 servings

As Williams students we must commend our rivals of Amherst College for contributing an exceptional recipe.

2 cups (500 ml) lightly packed fresh basil leaves
⅓ cup (80 ml) grated Parmesan cheese
3 cloves garlic, minced
½ teaspoon (3 ml) salt
½ teaspoon (3 ml) pepper

½ cup (125 ml) plus 1 teaspoon (5 ml) extra-virgin olive oil
½ of a 16-ounce (454 g) box penne pasta
3 boneless, skinless chicken half-breasts, cut into strips

Nutrition Per Serving	
Calories	586
Fat	31 g
Protein	30 g
Carbohydrates	44 g
Cholesterol	55 mg
Sodium	484 mg

1. In a food processor or blender, combine the basil, Parmesan, garlic, salt, and pepper; finely chop. Add ½ cup olive oil and blend the pesto sauce until smooth.
2. Bring a large pot of water to a boil. Add the pasta and cook until tender, about 8 minutes. Drain.
3. In a skillet, warm the remaining teaspoon of oil over medium heat. Add the chicken and sauté until cooked through (no pink shows in the middle), about 10 minutes.
4. Pour the pesto sauce over the drained pasta, and mix in the chicken. Serve warm or cold.

Mom's Tips

Quick Test

When frying or sautéing, to test whether the oil is hot enough, flick a drop of water into the skillet. If it spatters, the oil is ready to cook with. If not, keep heating.

Chicken with Artichoke

Makes 5 servings

For all you artichoke lovers out there. It's best served over rice or pasta.

Nutrition Per Serving

Calories	97
Fat	3 g
Protein	4 g
Carbohydrates	17 g
Cholesterol	0 mg
Sodium	278 mg

1 tablespoon (15 ml) extra-virgin olive oil
1 small yellow onion, chopped
1 green pepper, chopped
2 teaspoons (10 ml) dried basil
2 teaspoons (10 ml) minced garlic
1 14.5-ounce (411 g) can chopped, stewed tomatoes, drained

2 boneless, skinless chicken half-breasts, cut into bite-size chunks
½ teaspoon (3 ml) salt
1 teaspoon (5 ml) pepper
1 14-ounce (396 g) can artichoke hearts in water, drained

1. In a large skillet, warm the oil over medium heat. Add the onion and pepper and sauté for 5 minutes.
2. Stir in the basil, garlic, tomatoes, chicken, salt, and pepper. Reduce heat and simmer until the chicken is cooked through (no pink shows in the middle), about 15 minutes.
3. Add the artichoke hearts and continue simmering until heated through.

Apricot Chicken

Makes 4 servings

Leftovers of this recipe are great in vegetable stir-fries.

Nutrition Per Serving

Calories	164
Fat	2 g
Protein	27 g
Carbohydrates	9 g
Cholesterol	65 mg
Sodium	877 mg

4 boneless, skinless chicken half-breasts
2 tablespoons (30 ml) apricot jam

⅓ cup (80 ml) low-sodium soy sauce
1 tablespoon (15 ml) minced ginger

1. Mix the apricot jam, soy sauce, and ginger in a baking dish. Add the chicken, cover, and marinate in the refrigerator for at least 3 hours.
2. Preheat the oven to 350°F (180°C). Bake chicken for 30 minutes, or until cooked through (no pink shows in the middle).

Sesame Chicken

Makes 4 servings

This classic chicken recipe is good hot or cold.

4 boneless, skinless chicken
   half-breasts
4 tablespoons (60 ml) honey

3 tablespoons (45 ml)
   sesame seeds
1 teaspoon (5 ml) garlic powder
½ teaspoon (3 ml) pepper

1. Preheat the oven to 350°F (180°C).
2. Arrange the chicken in a single layer in a casserole dish. Warm the honey slightly in a microwave or small saucepan over low heat and brush evenly over chicken.
3. In a small bowl, combine the sesame seeds, garlic powder, and pepper, and sprinkle evenly over chicken. Bake uncovered for 30 minutes, or until the chicken is cooked through (no pink shows in the middle).

Nutrition Per Serving	
Calories	227
Fat	5 g
Protein	27 g
Carbohydrates	19 g
Cholesterol	65 mg
Sodium	74 mg

★Chicken Santa Fe

Makes 2 servings

From a friend at St. John's College in Santa Fe, New Mexico.

2 teaspoons (10 ml) extra-
   virgin olive oil
2 boneless, skinless chicken
   half-breasts
1 15-ounce (425 g) can black
   beans, rinsed and drained

1 medium tomato, chopped
½ green pepper, chopped
Hot sauce to taste
Ground cumin to taste
1 teaspoon (5 ml) chopped
   fresh cilantro (optional)

1. In a large skillet, warm the oil over medium heat. Add the chicken breasts and brown until cooked through (no pink shows in the middle), about 10–15 minutes.
2. In a saucepan over medium heat, warm the beans, tomato, and pepper. Season with hot sauce and cumin.
3. Place each chicken breast on a plate and smother with beans. Garnish with fresh cilantro and serve immediately.

Nutrition Per Serving	
Calories	892
Fat	9 g
Protein	71 g
Carbohydrates	133 g
Cholesterol	65 mg
Sodium	84 mg

★ Kelly's Chicken and Mushrooms

Makes 4 servings

This chicken dish is great with a plate of hot cooked rice.

Nutrition Per Serving

Calories	230
Fat	4 g
Protein	28 g
Carbohydrates	10 g
Cholesterol	65 mg
Sodium	80 mg

4 boneless, skinless chicken half-breasts
Flour for coating
2 teaspoons (10 ml) extra-virgin olive oil

2 cloves garlic, minced
1 onion, finely chopped
15 medium mushrooms, sliced
1 cup (250 ml) white wine
Salt and pepper to taste

1. Coat the chicken breasts with flour.
2. In a skillet, warm the oil over medium heat. Add the onion and garlic and sauté until the onions are translucent. Add the mushrooms and chicken to the pan, and cook until the chicken is cooked through (no pink shows in the middle).
3. Add the wine to the skillet. Continue stirring until the sauce in the pan thickens, repeatedly spooning it over the chicken breasts. Season with salt and pepper and serve each chicken breast with a little sauce drizzled over it.

Chicken Kabobs

Makes 4 servings

Also good with beef, fish, or tofu.

Nutrition Per Serving

Calories	226
Fat	3 g
Protein	30 g
Carbohydrates	21 g
Cholesterol	65 mg
Sodium	450 mg

4 boneless, skinless chicken half-breasts, cut into bite-size pieces
¾ cup (185 ml) teriyaki marinade (see page 126 for our recipe)
8 cherry tomatoes

1 yellow onion, cut into large wedges
1 green pepper, cut into large chunks
8 mushrooms

1. Marinate the chicken in the teriyaki sauce for 30 minutes in the refrigerator.
2. Thread the chicken, tomatoes, onion, green pepper, and mushrooms onto skewers, alternating ingredients.
3. Over a red-hot grill or under the broiler, cook the kabobs for 10–15 minutes, until the chicken is cooked through (no pink shows in the middle). Serve on or off the skewer over a bed of rice.

Chicken and Broccoli

Makes 4 servings

Serve this dish over a plate of rice.

3 cups (750 ml) chopped broccoli

2 carrots, chopped

2 cloves garlic, minced

2 tablespoons (30 ml) finely chopped yellow onion

1 teaspoon (5 ml) extra-virgin olive oil

4 boneless, skinless chicken half-breasts, cut into bite-size pieces

2 tablespoons (30 ml) teriyaki marinade, divided (see page 126 for our recipe)

Nutrition Per Serving	
Calories	224
Fat	3 g
Protein	40 g
Carbohydrates	7 g
Cholesterol	65 mg
Sodium	447 mg

1. In a large skillet, warm the oil over medium heat. Add all the vegetables and sauté until they begin to soften.
2. Add the chicken and 1 tablespoon teriyaki marinade. When the chicken begins to brown, add the second tablespoon of marinade. Cook for an additional 10–15 minutes, or until the chicken is cooked through (no pink shows in the middle). Serve immediately.

★Crispy Cracker Chicken

Makes 2 servings

A crispy alternative to fried chicken, courtesy of a friend at Washington University in St. Louis, Missouri.

2 boneless, skinless chicken half-breasts

1 egg white, beaten

½ cup (125 ml) crushed low-fat wheat crackers (like Wheat Thins)

½ cup (125 ml) grated Parmesan cheese

Nutrition Per Serving	
Calories	329
Fat	11 g
Protein	35 g
Carbohydrates	20 g
Cholesterol	75 mg
Sodium	570 mg

1. Preheat the oven to 350°F (180°C).
2. Rinse and pat dry the chicken breasts. Coat with the egg white.
3. In a wide, shallow bowl or platter, mix the crushed crackers and Parmesan. Roll the chicken breasts in the mixture until they are well coated.
4. Place the chicken in a pan and bake for about 35 minutes, until the chicken is cooked through (no pink shows in the middle) and the cracker coating is crispy.

Balsamic Mustard Chicken with Potatoes

Makes 4 servings

A substantial, warming dish good for cold, dreary days.

- 3 tablespoons (45 ml) Dijon mustard
- ¼ cup (60 ml) balsamic vinegar
- 2 tablespoons (30 ml) red wine vinegar
- 2 cloves garlic, minced
- 3 tablespoons (45 ml) finely chopped onion
- 2 tablespoons (45 ml) canola oil
- 4 boneless, skinless chicken half-breasts, cut into 1-inch (3 cm) strips
- 2 potatoes, very thinly sliced
- ½ cup (125 ml) low-sodium chicken broth

1. In a shallow dish, combine the mustard, vinegars, garlic, onion, and 1 tablespoon (15 ml) canola oil. Add the chicken, cover, and marinate in refrigerator for 30 minutes.
2. In a large pan, warm the remaining 1 tablespoon of oil over medium heat. Add the potato slices and cook until slightly crisp.
3. Add the chicken and marinade to the pan. Cook for 10–15 minutes, until the chicken is cooked through (no pink shows in the middle).
4. Add the chicken broth, and simmer for an additional 5 minutes, until the sauce reaches the desired consistency. Serve hot.

Flamin' Poultry

Makes 2 servings

The flamin' part depends on how generous you are with the hot sauce.

- 2 teaspoons (10 ml) butter
- ¼ cup (60 ml) hot sauce
- 2 boneless, skinless chicken half-breasts, cut into bite-size pieces

1. In a skillet, warm the butter over medium heat. Add the hot sauce and mix.
2. Add the chicken, stir to coat, and cover. Cook for about 10 minutes, or until cooked through (no pink shows in the middle).

Chicken with Olives and Tomato

Makes 4 servings

Serve this recipe on a bed of hot rice.

½ tablespoon (8 ml) extra-
virgin olive oil
4 boneless, skinless
chicken half-breasts
1 large yellow onion, finely
chopped

2 tablespoons (30 ml) red
wine vinegar
2 large tomatoes, chopped
⅔ cup (160 ml) sliced and
pitted black olives
Salt and pepper to taste

Nutrition Per Serving	
Calories	178
Fat	5 g
Protein	26 g
Carbohydrates	4 g
Cholesterol	65 mg
Sodium	275 mg

1. In a large skillet, warm the oil over medium heat. Add the chicken, cover, and cook for 12–15 minutes, until the chicken is cooked through (no pink shows in the middle). Remove the chicken from the pan and set aside.
2. Simmer the remaining ingredients in the chicken juice for 5 minutes. Return the chicken to the pan and heat through. Season with salt and pepper and serve hot.

KITCHEN QUICK TIP

7 Quick Sautés for Chicken

▸ Sauté with salsa or hot sauce and use the mixture as a tortilla filling.
▸ For fried chicken, coat chicken in egg, roll in flour, salt, and pepper and sauté in canola oil.
▸ Sauté chicken in a blend of white vinegar, soy sauce, ginger, and garlic for a quick teriyaki.
▸ Add some vegetables and call it a stir-fry.
▸ For a hot spinach salad, sauté chicken with mushrooms, onions, and garlic and serve on a bed of fresh spinach.
▸ If you have leftover rice, sauté chicken with chopped tomato, onion, garlic, white wine, and rosemary; add rice when chicken is cooked, heat through, and serve.
▸ Sauté chicken with salt and pepper. Serve it on a roll with lettuce and tomato for a hot chicken sandwich.

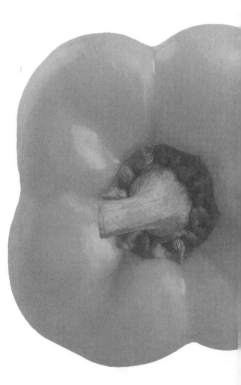

Chapter 9

Dishes for Meat-Lovers

We must admit that dining hall food did frighten us away from red meat for a brief time, but we've realized that when you're in control of buying, preparing, and cooking meat, it offers great variety. Barbecuing is fun, marinating is effortless, and there are an endless variety of seasonings and herbs to use.

It is important to make sure that your cut is fresh when you buy it. Check the date, look for discoloration (green = bad), and smell your purchase. When cooking any kind of meat, take heed of the "Handling Meats" cautions listed on page 20. As you probably know, raw meat can contain harmful bacteria, so all utensils, countertops, pans, bowls, and everything else that comes in contact with the raw meat, even the kitchen sink, should be carefully cleaned with soap and hot water. While this is a serious issue, don't let it scare you away. If you are careful and clean properly, you'll be fine. Enjoy our recipes and have fun creating your own.

Beef Stew

Makes 4 servings

This is great alone or over a bed of hot cooked rice. If the stew seems too dry to your taste, you can add some beef broth. You can use any kind of beer you prefer (including nonalcoholic).

1 pound (450 g) chuck steak, cut into 1-inch (2-cm) cubes
1 teaspoon (5 ml) extra-virgin olive oil
½ cup (125 ml) chopped onion
½ cup (125 ml) chopped green pepper
2 cups (500 ml) beer
Oregano to taste
Basil to taste

Salt and pepper to taste
1 cube beef bouillon
1¼ cup (310 ml) water
2 tablespoons (30 ml) all-purpose flour
½ cup (125 ml) chopped carrots
1 cup (250 ml) chopped potatoes

Nutrition Per Serving	
Calories	332
Fat	19 g
Protein	19 g
Carbohydrates	13 g
Cholesterol	66 mg
Sodium	289 mg

1. In a large pot over medium heat, brown the steak cubes in the oil. Be careful not to overcook. Add the onion and green pepper. Reduce heat, cover, and simmer for 5 minutes.
2. Add the beer. Season with oregano, basil, salt, and pepper. Bring to a boil; stir in the bouillon and 1 cup of water. Reduce heat, cover, and simmer, stirring occasionally, for 1 hour or until the beef is tender.
3. In a small cup, mix the flour with ¼ cup of water, and then stir the mixture into the stew (this will prevent the flour from getting lumpy when added). Add the carrots and potatoes. Cover and simmer, stirring occasionally, for 40 minutes or until the vegetables are tender.

Tacos

Makes 4 servings

Nutrition Per Serving

Calories	369
Fat	24 g
Protein	23 g
Carbohydrates	14 g
Cholesterol	78 mg
Sodium	156 mg

This recipe includes the basics of any good taco. However, for more variety and a healthier palette, consider adding to the buffet table grilled or roasted vegetables of all sorts — green and red peppers, onions, zucchini, and mushrooms are good choices. It's a great way to use up leftover vegetables, as well as a great excuse for making extra vegetables the night before.

1 **pound (450 g) lean ground beef**	½ **cup (125 ml) chopped lettuce**
8 **taco shells**	**Salsa to taste**
1 **tomato, diced**	**Hot sauce to taste**

1. In a nonstick skillet, cook the ground beef over medium-high heat until browned.
2. Transfer the beef to a plate. Serve buffet-style with the taco shells, tomato, lettuce, salsa, and hot sauce.

Beef Burritos

Makes 4 servings

Nutrition Per Serving

Calories	499
Fat	25 g
Protein	28 g
Carbohydrates	40 g
Cholesterol	78 mg
Sodium	413 mg

Like the taco recipe above, this dish is even better with whatever leftover grilled or roasted vegetables you have on hand.

1 **pound (450 g) lean ground beef**	8 **flour tortillas**
1 **teaspoon (5 ml) hot sauce**	1 **tomato, diced**
1 **teaspoon (5 ml) cayenne**	½ **cup (125 ml) chopped lettuce**
1 **teaspoon (5 ml) chili powder**	**Salsa to taste**

1. In a skillet over medium-high heat, cook the beef, hot sauce, cayenne, and chili powder until the beef is browned.
2. Serve the beef, tortillas, tomato, lettuce, and salsa on separate plates, buffet-style. To make a burrito, place a couple of spoonfuls of ingredients in the center of a tortilla. Fold one edge up to make a bottom lip over the filling, then fold the sides in to overlap in the center, making a secure basket for the filling.

Beef Stir-Fry

Makes 4 servings

This recipe comes compliments of a friend at Rutgers University in New Brunswick, New Jersey.

When marinating the beef for this recipe, there should be a small puddle of soy sauce at the bottom on the bowl. If there isn't, add a little more soy sauce. Serve the stir-fry alone or with sticky rice or couscous. It's also good with chicken instead of beef, or different vegetables instead of broccoli. Use whatever's in the refrigerator — it's all good.

Nutrition Per Serving	
Calories	508
Fat	31 g
Protein	37 g
Carbohydrates	19 g
Cholesterol	117 mg
Sodium	1,740 mg

⅔ cup (160 ml) low-sodium soy sauce
2 scallions, sliced
1 medium onion, chopped
Pepper to taste
2 teaspoons (10 ml) brown sugar

1½ pounds (675 g) lean beef, cut into bite-size pieces
2 tablespoons (30 ml) sesame oil
4 cups (1 l) chopped broccoli

1. In a large bowl, combine the soy sauce, scallions, onion, pepper, and brown sugar. Add the beef and marinate for 10 minutes.
2. In a large wok or skillet over medium heat, warm the oil. Add the beef, marinade, and broccoli, and sauté until the meat is cooked to your liking, stirring occasionally. Add a little water if there's not enough liquid in the pan.

KITCHEN QUICK TIP

Keep It Lean

The nutritional analyses for these recipes assume that all of the fat from the ground beef stays with it as it is cooked and served. To cut down on fat, drain the skillet after cooking, and pat the cooked ground beef with a paper towel to absorb excess grease. You won't be able to get rid of all of it, but you can make a sizable dent.

Turkey Burgers

Makes 4 servings

To make sure the burgers are fully cooked, cut one burger open to its middle. If it's still pink, keep cooking.

1½ pounds (675 g) lean ground turkey
¼ cup (60 ml) whole wheat bread crumbs
2 cloves garlic, minced

1 teaspoon (5 ml) hot sauce (optional)
Pepper to taste
1 teaspoon (5 ml) extra-virgin olive oil

1. In a large bowl, combine the turkey, bread crumbs, garlic, hot sauce, and pepper, and mix well with your hands. Form the mixture into four patties.
2. In a skillet, warm the oil over medium heat. Cook the burgers in the oil for 5 minutes per side, or until they're done.

Mom's Tips

Burger Tips

► In most recipes, ground turkey is a great substitute for ground beef. Lean ground turkey usually contains less fat than lean ground beef.

► We didn't use egg in our burger recipes because we think it adds unnecessary bad stuff (like cholesterol). But that comes with a price tag: These burgers may crumble a little if you're not careful with them. If you want burgers that are easier to handle and you don't mind a little extra cholesterol, try adding an egg or two (or just their whites) to these recipes.

► When freezing leftover raw ground beef, mold it into hamburger patties first. You can then defrost only the amount you need for the particular meal you will be preparing.

Stan's Southern Burger

Makes 4 servings

To make your own bread crumbs, toast a slice of stale bread, then toss it in the blender for a few seconds. No blender? Just use a knife to scrape the toast into crumbs.

1¼ pounds (568 g) lean
    ground beef
¼ cup (60 ml) whole wheat
    bread crumbs

2 medium mushrooms, diced
1 tablespoon (15 ml) salsa
1 teaspoon (5 ml) hot sauce

Nutrition Per Serving	
Calories	363
Fat	25 g
Protein	28 g
Carbohydrates	6 g
Cholesterol	98 mg
Sodium	179 mg

1. Prepare the grill.
2. Combine all the ingredients in a large bowl and mix thoroughly with hands. Form the mixture into four patties.
3. Grill for about 4 minutes per side, until the burgers are done to your satisfaction.

Steak à l'Orange

Makes 4 servings

An easy preparation for a steak dinner.

2 oranges
2 teaspoons (10 ml) extra-
    virgin olive oil

1 teaspoon (5 ml) chili powder
4 8-ounce (230 g) beefsteaks
Salt and pepper to taste

Nutrition Per Serving	
Calories	515
Fat	35 g
Protein	42 g
Carbohydrates	8 g
Cholesterol	144 mg
Sodium	122 mg

1. Prepare the grill or preheat the broiler.
2. Grate the rind from the oranges. Combine orange rind with oil and 1 teaspoon chili powder. Mix well. Spread the orange mixture evenly over both sides of each steak.
3. Grill or broil the steaks for 5 minutes on each side or to desired doneness.
4. Squeeze some orange juice over the top of each steak. Season with salt and pepper.

Flank Steak

Makes 4 servings

Nutrition Per Serving

Calories	413
Fat	18 g
Protein	46 g
Carbohydrates	16 g
Cholesterol	87 mg
Sodium	924 mg

The simple marinade used here, from the University of Colorado at Boulder, is also very tasty with chicken or salmon.

⅔ cup (160 ml) low-sodium soy sauce

4 tablespoons (60 ml) brown sugar

2 teaspoons (10 ml) minced fresh ginger

1½ pounds (675 g) flank steak

1. In a shallow dish, combine the soy sauce, brown sugar, and ginger. Marinate the steak in the mixture for at least 3 hours in the refrigerator.
2. Preheat the broiler. Remove the steak from the marinade and broil for about 5 minutes per side, until it's done to your satisfaction. For a more intense flavor, you can pan-cook the steak in the marinade.

Chili con Carne

Makes 6 servings

Nutrition Per Serving

Calories	311
Fat	15 g
Protein	21 g
Carbohydrates	25 g
Cholesterol	52 mg
Sodium	706 mg

The flavor of this recipe will improve with age, so save the extras for leftovers.

½ cup (125 ml) chopped onion

1 teaspoon (5 ml) extra-virgin olive oil

2 cloves garlic, minced

2 15-ounce (425 g) cans chopped tomatoes, drained

2 15-ounce (425 g) cans kidney beans, drained

2 tablespoons (30 ml) chili powder

1 tablespoon (15 ml) sugar

Salt and pepper to taste

1 pound (450 g) lean ground beef

A small pinch of nutmeg

1 bay leaf

1. In a large pot, warm the oil over medium heat. Add the onion and garlic and sauté until the onions are tender. Add the tomatoes, beans, chili powder, sugar, salt, pepper, nutmeg, and bay leaf, and stir well. Reduce heat to low and let simmer.
2. In a separate pan over medium heat, brown the beef. Drain the fat from the pan and add the beef to the chili. Allow to simmer for 1½ hours.

Uncle J's Meat Loaf

Makes 4 servings

Make a little extra of this recipe. It tastes good cold and makes a great sandwich that will really fill you up. It's a great way to plan ahead if you know you've got a hectic week coming up.

Nutrition Per Serving

Calories	280
Fat	16 g
Protein	20 g
Carbohydrates	13 g
Cholesterol	104 mg
Sodium	330 mg

¼ cup (60 ml) skim milk
1 slice whole wheat bread
½ onion, chopped
¾ pound (338 g) lean
  ground beef
1 egg, beaten

¼ cup (60 ml) chopped fresh
  parsley
¼ cup (60 ml) ketchup
½ teaspoon (3 ml) hot sauce
  Salt and pepper to taste

1. Preheat the oven to 350°F (180°C).
2. Pour the milk into a small bowl and place the bread on top. When most of the milk has been absorbed by the bread (about 3–4 minutes) add the onion, beef, egg, parsley, ketchup, hot sauce, salt, and pepper. Mix with your hands until no chunks of bread are visible.
3. Pat the mixture into a small casserole dish and bake for 1 hour.
4. Remove from the oven and cool for 10 minutes. Carefully drain the liquid from dish, making sure not to lose the loaf to the sink. Serve in slices.

Adding Fiber

Adding oats to a meat loaf provides greater fiber content and won't affect the flavor. Try adding a handful or two to each loaf.

★ Mexican Lasagna

Makes 6 servings

This one will take a little extra time, but it's worth it.

Mom's Tips

Storing Cheese

When returning an opened package of cheese to the refrigerator, remove the original wrapping and place the cheese in an airtight plastic bag. It may seem wasteful to use so much plastic, but you can always recycle the bags, and they will keep your cheese from getting stale and hard.

1 large onion, chopped
½ green pepper, chopped
2 teaspoons (10 ml) extra-virgin olive oil
3 cloves garlic, minced
1¼ pounds (568 g) lean ground beef
2 tablespoons (30 ml) chopped jalapeño pepper
2 cups (500 ml) tomato sauce

1½ cups (375 ml) low-sodium beef broth
1 tablespoon (15 ml) flour
Salt to taste
6 small flour tortillas, cut into three strips each
3 tablespoons (45 ml) finely chopped cilantro (optional)
2 cups (500 ml) shredded low-fat cheddar cheese

1. Preheat the oven to 350°F (180°C).
2. In a large pan, warm the oil over medium heat. Add the onion and green pepper and sauté until the onion becomes translucent. Add the garlic and cook an additional 2 minutes.
3. Add the beef and cook until brown. Stir in the jalapeño, tomato sauce, and half of the beef broth. Cover and let simmer.
4. In a bowl, gradually mix the flour with the remaining beef broth; add to the beef mixture. Simmer until the sauce thickens. Remove from heat, add the cilantro, and stir well.
5. Fill a casserole dish with the sauce, cheese, and tortillas in alternating layers, beginning with a thin sauce layer and ending with a cheese layer. Bake for 15–20 minutes or until heated through.

★ Real Sloppy Sloppy Joe

Makes 4 servings

A childhood classic dressed up for an older crowd.

1½ pounds (675 g) lean ground beef
½ yellow onion, finely chopped
1 clove garlic, minced
½ cup (125 ml) ketchup
¼ cup (60 ml) crushed tomatoes (or tomato sauce)
1 tablespoon (15 ml) red wine vinegar
2 tablespoons (30 ml) Worcestershire sauce
2 teaspoons (10 ml) hot sauce
Salt and pepper to taste
4 hamburger buns

Nutrition Per Serving	
Calories	536
Fat	30 g
Protein	37 g
Carbohydrates	31 g
Cholesterol	118 mg
Sodium	779 mg

1. In a nonstick skillet over medium heat, brown the beef with the onion and garlic. Drain excess fat.
2. Add the ketchup, crushed tomatoes, vinegar, Worcestershire sauce, hot sauce, and salt and pepper to taste. Stir well and simmer for 5 minutes.
3. While the beef mixture is simmering, toast the hamburger buns.
4. Arrange the buns face-up on plates. Ladle a healthy portion of the beef mixture over each and serve immediately.

Beef Stroganoff

Makes 4 servings

A great hot dish for cold winter nights.

½ of a 16-ounce (454 g) package egg noodles
1¼ pound (568 g) top round beef, cut into small chunks
¼ cup (60 ml) sliced onions
1 tablespoon (15 ml) flour
1 clove garlic, minced
8 fresh mushrooms, sliced
½ cup (125 ml) low-sodium chicken broth
½ cup (125 ml) nonfat sour cream
Salt and pepper to taste

1. Bring a pot of water to a boil. Add the noodles and cook until tender, about 8–10 minutes. Drain and set aside.
2. In a skillet over medium heat, cook the beef and onions. As the beef begins to brown, stir in the flour so that it coats the beef.
3. Stir in the garlic, mushrooms, chicken broth, and sour cream. Cook until the sauce is an even consistency and the mushrooms are soft. Add salt and pepper. Serve over egg noodles.

Ham in Cider-Raisin Sauce

Makes 4 servings

You can use either hard or sweet cider for this recipe.

1½ pounds (680 g) lean hamsteak, sliced in four even pieces
2 teaspoons (10 ml) extra-virgin olive oil
2 tablespoons (30 ml) butter
2 tablespoons (30 ml) flour
1½ cups (375 ml) cider
½ cup (125 ml) raisins
1 tablespoon (15 ml) sugar
1 teaspoon (5 ml) Dijon mustard

1. In a large skillet, warm the oil over medium heat. Add the ham and cook for about 4 minutes per side, or until it's done to your satisfaction. Once done, you may want to pat the ham with paper towels to absorb some of the excess grease.
2. In a saucepan, melt the butter. Add the flour and stir. Stir in the cider, raisins, sugar, and mustard. Bring to a boil. Reduce heat and simmer for 5 minutes or until thickened.
3. Pour the sauce evenly over the ham steaks and serve.

Sweet and Sour Pork

Makes 4 servings

Serve over rice or couscous, making sure to get every last drop of sauce out of the pan and onto your plate.

1 tablespoon (15 ml) butter
1 pound (454 g) lean pork, cut into small cubes
1 medium onion, chopped
1½ cups (375 ml) water
2 tablespoons (30 ml) brown sugar, firmly packed
¼ cup (60 ml) raisins
1 medium tomato, diced
1 sprig fresh rosemary
1 tablespoon (15 ml) red wine vinegar

Nutrition Per Serving	
Calories	288
Fat	17 g
Protein	16 g
Carbohydrates	17 g
Cholesterol	67 mg
Sodium	80 mg

1. In a saucepan, melt the butter over medium heat. Add the pork cubes and onion and sauté for 5 minutes, until the pork is cooked through.
2. Add the water, brown sugar, raisins, tomato, and rosemary. Cover and cook for 10 minutes.
3. Add the red wine vinegar. Bring to a boil and simmer for about 5 minutes, stirring often, until the sauce has been reduced by about half. Serve immediately.

Teriyaki Pork Chops

Makes 4 servings

When broiling pork in the oven, place a foil-lined baking sheet on the rack below to catch the juices dripping from the chops.

1½ cups (375 ml) teriyaki marinade (see page 126 for our recipe)
4 pork chops (about 1½ pounds, or 680 g, total)

Nutrition Per Serving	
Calories	239
Fat	15 g
Protein	24 g
Carbohydrates	1 g
Cholesterol	74 mg
Sodium	403 mg

1. Pour the teriyaki marinade into a shallow dish and place pork chops on top. Marinate in the refrigerator for about 1½ hours.
2. Preheat the broiler or prepare the grill. Take the chops out of the marinade and place them on the top rack of oven or on the grill. Cook for about 5–8 minutes on each side, or to the desired doneness. (When cooked through, the meat will not be pink in the middle.)

Chapter 10

Side Dishes & Sauces

Many people, especially students and others with little time, are of the opinion that a single dish can suffice as a full meal. We contest — side dishes can elevate an everyday meal from good to great. Contrasts in taste and texture, nutritional benefits, and even aesthetics will prove to be worth the small amount of time and energy necessary to prepare these dishes. And your parents will be happy to know that you're eating a well-balanced meal.

Sauces and dressings are a great way to spice up a side dish or main meal or to give new life to leftovers. You'll find all of the recipes easy to prepare, but don't feel restricted by our suggestions. There's plenty of room to be creative and discover a combination that suits your own particular tastes.

Mashed Potatoes

Makes 4 servings

If you're trying to cut down on fat, omit the butter in this recipe. An easy, low-fat way to spice up mashed potatoes is to add herbs, such as chives or parsley, and nonfat sour cream or plain yogurt.

Nutrition Per Serving	
Calories	124
Fat	2 g
Protein	3 g
Carbohydrates	24 g
Cholesterol	5 mg
Sodium	29 mg

- 2 large potatoes, peeled and quartered
- 2 teaspoons (10 ml) butter
- 1 tablespoon (15 ml) skim milk
- Salt and pepper to taste

1. Bring a large pot of water to a boil. Add the potatoes and boil until soft, about 20–30 minutes. Drain.
2. In a large mixing bowl, mash the potatoes with a fork (or a potato masher, if you own one). Add the butter, milk, and salt and pepper, and continue mashing until the potatoes reach the desired consistency.

Hash Browns

Makes 4 servings

If you have leftovers from this recipe, try folding them into an omelette with some green peppers and tomatoes.

Nutrition Per Serving	
Calories	137
Fat	2 g
Protein	3 g
Carbohydrates	27 g
Cholesterol	5 mg
Sodium	28 mg

- 2 large potatoes, scrubbed and diced
- 2 teaspoons (10 ml) butter
- 1 small onion, chopped

1. Bring a medium pot of water to a boil. Add the potatoes and cook until tender, about 10 minutes.
2. In a large skillet, melt the butter over low heat. Add the potatoes and onion, cover, and cook for 10 minutes. Remove the cover, turn heat to high, and brown the potatoes until done to your satisfaction.

Twice-Baked Potatoes

Makes 4 servings

Nutrition Per Serving

Calories	222
Fat	5 g
Protein	18 g
Carbohydrates	27 g
Cholesterol	62 mg
Sodium	347 mg

Although this recipe doesn't require much from the chef, it does require some cooking time, so remember to plan ahead.

2 medium baking potatoes
1 cup (250 ml) nonfat cottage cheese
1 hard-boiled egg, finely chopped
1 fresh tomato, diced
1½ tablespoons (23 ml) Dijon mustard

Salt to taste
1½ teaspoons (8 ml) dried dill
¾ cup (185 ml) shredded low-fat cheddar cheese
¼ teaspoon (1 ml) pepper

1. Preheat the oven to 400°F (205°C).
2. Scrub the potatoes and remove the eyes, then pierce the skin all over with a fork. Bake directly on the oven rack for approximately 1 hour. Remove potatoes and lower the oven temperature to 325°F (165°C). Allow the potatoes to cool until you can handle them comfortably.
3. Slice the potatoes in half lengthwise. Scoop out the insides of the potatoes and place in a mixing bowl, so that you are left with four small boats. Set the boats aside.
4. Combine the potato filling with the cottage cheese, egg, tomato, mustard, salt, dill, cheese, and pepper, and mix thoroughly.
5. Place the potato-skin boats on a cookie sheet and overstuff them with the mixture. Bake for an additional 35 minutes. Serve immediately.

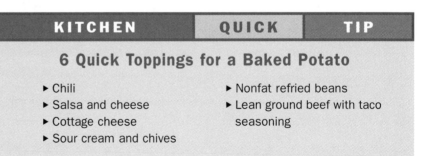

KITCHEN QUICK TIP

6 Quick Toppings for a Baked Potato

- Chili
- Salsa and cheese
- Cottage cheese
- Sour cream and chives

- Nonfat refried beans
- Lean ground beef with taco seasoning

Apple Sweet Potato

Makes 4 servings

You can use either hard or sweet cider for this recipe.

2 large sweet potatoes, peeled
   and sliced ¼-inch thick
2 medium Granny Smith apples,
   peeled, cored, and sliced
2 teaspoons (15 ml) butter

3 tablespoons (45 ml) honey
½ tablespoon (8 ml) lemon juice
  Salt to taste
¼ cup (60 ml) cider

Nutrition Per Serving	
Calories	153
Fat	2 g
Protein	3 g
Carbohydrates	34 g
Cholesterol	5 mg
Sodium	28 mg

1. Preheat the oven to 350°F (180°C).
2. In a small saucepan combine the butter, honey, and lemon juice. Cook over low heat until thoroughly mixed.
3. Arrange the potato and apple slices in a shallow baking dish. Drizzle about half of the sauce over the slices. Bake for 45 minutes, basting often with remaining sauce and any sauce that collects at the bottom of the baking dish.

Applesauce

Makes 4 servings

This recipe is also good with a touch of ginger.

½ cup (125 ml) water
4 apples, peeled, cored, and
  sliced (we recommend
  Macintosh)

½ teaspoon cinnamon
  A pinch of nutmeg

Nutrition Per Serving	
Calories	62
Fat	0 g
Protein	0 g
Carbohydrates	16 g
Cholesterol	0 mg
Sodium	0 mg

1. In a saucepan, bring the water to a boil. Add the apple slices, cover, and cook over low heat for about 10 minutes. Then turn heat up to medium and cook, covered, for about 20 minutes more, or until the apples are soft.
2. Remove from heat and, with a fork or spoon, mash the apples until they reach an even consistency. Season with cinnamon and nutmeg.

★ Spaghetti Squash with Cinnamon

Makes 4 servings

This takes a bit of time, but not much attention.

Nutrition Per Serving

Calories	36
Fat	3 g
Protein	0 g
Carbohydrates	3 g
Cholesterol	8 mg
Sodium	168 mg

1 **large (or 2 small) spaghetti squash, halved and seeded**
1 **tablespoon (15 ml) butter**
¼ **teaspoon (1 ml) salt**
¼ **teaspoon (1 ml) cinnamon**

1. Preheat the oven 350°F (180°C).
2. Halve the squash and place face down on a cookie sheet. Bake for 30 minutes, or until soft.
3. Scrape out the insides of the squash with a fork so the strands begin to separate. Place the pulp in an ovenproof dish. Mix in the butter, salt, and cinnamon.
4. Bake for an additional 15 minutes. Serve hot.

Steamed Asparagus

Makes 4 servings

This makes a wonderful side dish for a great many recipes.

Nutrition Per Serving

Calories	66
Fat	3 g
Protein	4 g
Carbohydrates	7 g
Cholesterol	8 mg
Sodium	32 mg

¼ **cup (60 ml) water**
16 **medium stalks asparagus**
1 **tablespoon (15 ml) butter**
1 **teaspoon (5 ml) lemon juice**

1. In a saucepan, bring the water to a boil. Add the asparagus and cook until the asparagus is tender, about 7–8 minutes.
2. Drain the asparagus and set on a serving dish. Sprinkle with slivers of butter and lemon juice.

✿ ★ ⏱ Steamed Cabbage

Makes 4 servings

This may not sound like much, but it is one of the cheapest things you can buy, it's healthy, and it even tastes good.

½ head cabbage, shredded
Salt and pepper to taste

1. Fill a pot with ¼ inch (½ cm) of water and bring to a boil. Add the cabbage and steam for about 10 minutes, or until tender. Drain.
2. Season with salt and pepper. Serve hot.

Nutrition Per Serving	
Calories	16
Fat	0 g
Protein	1 g
Carbohydrates	3 g
Cholesterol	0 mg
Sodium	18 mg

✿ ⏱ Glazed Carrots

Makes 4 servings

A fast and healthy side dish!

¼ cup (60 ml) water
3 cups (500 ml) chopped carrots

1 teaspoon (5 ml) butter
1 tablespoon (15 ml) honey
Nutmeg to taste

1. In a medium saucepan, bring the water to a boil. Add the carrots and cook, covered, over medium heat for 10–15 minutes, until the carrots are tender. Drain.
2. Add the honey and butter to the hot saucepan, and stir until they are melted together. Add the carrots and gently toss. Sprinkle with nutmeg.

Nutrition Per Serving	
Calories	56
Fat	1 g
Protein	1 g
Carbohydrates	12 g
Cholesterol	3 mg
Sodium	36 mg

★Grated Zucchini

Makes 4 servings

Nutrition Per Serving

Calories	22
Fat	1 g
Protein	1 g
Carbohydrates	3 g
Cholesterol	3 mg
Sodium	279 mg

When summertime hits and your local grocery is practically giving zucchini away, this recipe will cost next to nothing to prepare.

2½ cups (625 ml) packed grated zucchini
3 tablespoons (45 ml) finely chopped onion

1 teaspoon (5 ml) butter
½ teaspoon (3 ml) salt, plus extra for seasoning
Pepper to taste

1. Sprinkle ½ teaspoon of the salt over the zucchini and leave it in a strainer for at least 1 hour, and longer if possible. Then squeeze out the excess water with your hands.
2. In a skillet, melt the butter over medium heat. Add the onion and zucchini and sauté for about 5 minutes, until the onion is translucent. Season with salt and pepper and serve.

Grilled Eggplant

Makes 4 servings

Nutrition Per Serving

Calories	86
Fat	7 g
Protein	1 g
Carbohydrates	6 g
Cholesterol	0 mg
Sodium	137 mg

For a homemade vegetable marinade, see our recipe page 126.

1 medium eggplant
Vegetable marinade

1. Peel the eggplant, then slice into ½-inch steaks. Soak in marinade for 1 hour.
2. Preheat the broiler.
3. Place the slices on a rack and broil until hot and soft, about 5 minutes per side.

Amy's Black-Eyed Peas

Makes 4 servings

A friend at Dartmouth College in Hanover, New Hampshire, gave us this recipe.

1 cup (250 ml) black-eyed peas
1 clove garlic, minced
⅓ cup (80 ml) fresh lemon juice
2 teaspoons (10 ml) dried mint
½ teaspoon (3 ml) salt

Nutrition Per Serving	
Calories	173
Fat	1 g
Protein	11 g
Carbohydrates	32 g
Cholesterol	0 mg
Sodium	536 mg

1. Prepare the black-eyed peas according to the package directions, making sure they are cooked through. Drain and place in a medium bowl. Cover and refrigerate until chilled.
2. Add the remaining ingredients to the bowl. Mix well and serve cold.

Balsamic Tomatoes

Makes 4 servings

When you tire of green salads, give this recipe a try.

2 medium tomatoes, cut into thick slices
½ medium onion, chopped
3 tablespoons (45 ml) balsamic vinegar
2 teaspoons (10 ml) extra-virgin olive oil
Pepper to taste

Nutrition Per Serving	
Calories	28
Fat	2 g
Protein	0 g
Carbohydrates	2 g
Cholesterol	0 mg
Sodium	1 mg

1. Arrange the tomato slices on a plate and sprinkle with the onion.
2. Drizzle the vinegar and oil over the tomatoes, and season with pepper. Allow to marinate for at least 5 minutes before serving.

Sweet Acorn Squash

Makes 4 servings

Nutrition Per Serving

Calories	68
Fat	2 g
Protein	1 g
Carbohydrates	13 g
Cholesterol	5 mg
Sodium	24 mg

Mom's Tips

Quick Cooking

To reduce the cooking time for this recipe, before baking you can place the cut pieces of squash in a microwave-safe dish and microwave on high for 8 minutes. This should reduce the oven cooking time to about 15 minutes.

This is a great fall dish. It's great with a variety of squashes — we recommend acorn or butternut.

2 small acorn squash (or 1 large squash — approximately ¼ pound, or 113 g, per person)

2 teaspoons (10 ml) butter
4 teaspoons (20 ml) brown sugar

1. Preheat the oven to 350°F (180°C).
2. Cut the squash into halves and scoop out the seeds. (If you're using a large squash, cut it into quarters.)
3. With a fork, poke holes in the flesh of the squash. Drop ½ teaspoon (3 ml) of butter and 1 teaspoon (5 ml) of sugar into the center of each piece.
4. Place the squash face up in a baking pan. Cover with aluminum foil and bake until soft, approximately 40 minutes.

Broccoli with Onions and Soy Sauce

Makes 4 servings

This recipe is great served over rice.

4 cups (1 l) chopped broccoli
1 teaspoon (5 ml) sesame oil
1 onion, chopped

⅓ cup (80 ml) low-sodium soy sauce

1. Place the broccoli in a large pot and fill with ¼ to ½ inch (about 1 cm) of water. Bring to a boil, reduce heat, and steam for 3–4 minutes (you don't want it to be fully cooked).
2. In a large pan over medium heat, warm the oil. Add the onion and sauté until it's just beginning to become translucent. Then add the broccoli and soy sauce and cook, stirring often, for 5 minutes.

Nutrition Per Serving	
Calories	62
Fat	1 g
Protein	4 g
Carbohydrates	10 g
Cholesterol	0 mg
Sodium	825 mg

KITCHEN QUICK TIP

6 Quick Recipes for Rice

▸ Add dry chicken soup mix to the boiling water; when rice is cooked, mix in some leftover cooked chicken and serve when heated through.

▸ Add onion soup mix to the boiling water, then add sautéed mushrooms just before serving.

▸ Cook rice in low-sodium vegetable broth, and add your choice of vegetables.

▸ Mix salsa in with cooked rice, with or without cheese.

▸ Stir in curry powder and leftover cooked chicken.

▸ For quick red beans and rice, heat up some canned red beans. Stir in onions, celery, green pepper, garlic, and oregano to taste. Serve over white rice.

Island Teriyaki Marinade

Makes 4 servings

Nutrition Per Serving	
Calories	118
Fat	5 g
Protein	2 g
Carbohydrates	17 g
Cholesterol	0 mg
Sodium	1,206 mg

You can use this marinade for meats, fish, vegetables, and just about anything else you can think of. Depending on the thickness of the food, you'll want to marinate for at least one or two hours before cooking.

- ½ cup (125 ml) low-sodium soy sauce
- ¼ cup (60 ml) packed brown sugar
- 1½ tablespoons (23 ml) extra-virgin olive oil
- 1 tablespoon (15 ml) grated fresh ginger
- ¼ teaspoon (1 ml) pepper
- 2 cloves garlic, minced

Combine all the ingredients and mix well. This recipe will keep for 3–4 weeks if kept covered in the refrigerator.

Vegetable Marinade

Makes 4 servings

Nutrition Per Serving	
Calories	125
Fat	13 g
Protein	0 g
Carbohydrates	2 g
Cholesterol	0 mg
Sodium	268 mg

Use this marinade for vegetables such as zucchini, eggplant, and mushrooms.

- ¼ cup (125 ml) extra-virgin olive oil
- ¼ cup (60 ml) balsamic vinegar
- 1 tablespoon (15 ml) water
- 1 clove garlic, minced
- 1 teaspoon (5 ml) dried oregano
- ½ teaspoon (3 ml) pepper
- ¼ teaspoon (3 ml) salt

Combine all the ingredients and stir well.

Apple Cinnamon Puree

Makes 6 servings

Serve over plain fruit salads or as a summer dip for sliced fruit.

1 medium apple, peeled and chopped
⅓ cup (80 ml) skim milk
⅔ cup (160 ml) nonfat plain yogurt

2 teaspoons (10 ml) sugar
2 teaspoons (10 ml) cinnamon

Nutrition Per Serving	
Calories	33
Fat	0 g
Protein	4 g
Carbohydrates	6 g
Cholesterol	1 mg
Sodium	27 mg

In a blender, puree all the ingredients until smooth.

★ Mom's BBQ Sauce

Makes 10 servings

Tastes great on chicken!

1 small yellow onion, finely chopped
½ tablespoon (8 ml) extra-virgin olive oil
1 tablespoon (15 ml) Worcestershire sauce
2 tablespoons (30 ml) red wine vinegar

2 tablespoons (30 ml) lemon juice
⅔ cup (160 ml) ketchup
1 tablespoon (15 ml) mustard
1 teaspoon (5 ml) hot sauce
A pinch of salt
½ teaspoon (3 ml) pepper

Nutrition Per Serving	
Calories	33
Fat	1 g
Protein	0 g
Carbohydrates	7 g
Cholesterol	0 mg
Sodium	238 mg

1. In a medium saucepan, warm the oil over medium heat. Add the onion and sauté until translucent.
2. Add the remaining ingredients; stir well. Simmer about 15 minutes, stirring occasionally.

Chicken Gravy

Makes 8 servings

Nutrition Per Serving

Calories	9
Fat	0 g
Protein	2 g
Carbohydrates	2 g
Cholesterol	0 mg
Sodium	65 mg

This also works well for beef — just switch the broth.

2 tablespoons (30 ml) flour

1 cup (250 ml) low-sodium chicken broth

In a saucepan, slowly whisk the flour into the broth until it reaches an even consistency. Bring the broth to a boil, reduce heat, and simmer, stirring often, until the sauce thickens.

Gravy Tips

▶ The flour or corn starch in your gravy should be mixed with cold liquid — they get lumpy when mixed with hot liquid. If the gravy or sauce is already hot, mix the flour with a bit of cold water before adding.

▶ If you need to thicken a gravy or cream sauce, try adding a little flour or corn starch. Stir it into the sauce until it has been absorbed.

▶ If you overspice a gravy, add a peeled raw potato to absorb some of the seasoning. Let soak for a little while, then remove and discard.

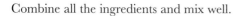 # Basic Oil and Vinegar Dressing

Makes 6 servings

An old favorite.

⅓ cup (80 ml) balsamic
  vinegar
¼ cup (60 ml) water
¼ cup (60 ml) extra-virgin
  olive oil

1 clove garlic, minced
½ teaspoon (3 ml) oregano
½ teaspoon (3 ml) basil
  Salt and pepper to taste

Nutrition Per Serving	
Calories	82
Fat	9 g
Protein	0 g
Carbohydrates	1 g
Cholesterol	0 mg
Sodium	1 mg

Combine all the ingredients and mix well.

Italian Dressing

Makes 4 servings

A standard dressing at any table — everyone should be familiar with this one.

2 tablespoons (30 ml) white-wine vinegar	**¼ cup (60 ml) extra-virgin olive oil**
½ teaspoon (3 ml) Dijon mustard	**3 tablespoons (45 ml) water**
1 clove garlic, minced	**1 teaspoon (5 ml) dried oregano**
Salt and pepper to taste	

Combine all the ingredients and mix well.

Nutrition Per Serving

Calories	123
Fat	14 g
Protein	0 g
Carbohydrates	1 g
Cholesterol	0 mg
Sodium	9 mg

Blue Cheese Dressing

Makes 6 servings

Good on salads and as a dip for vegetables.

¼ cup (60 ml) crumbled blue cheese	**½ clove garlic, minced**
½ cup (125 ml) nonfat plain yogurt	**½ teaspoon (3 ml) Dijon mustard**

Cream half of the cheese in a small bowl. Mix in the yogurt, garlic, and mustard. Add the remaining cheese and stir well.

Nutrition Per Serving

Calories	31
Fat	2 g
Protein	2 g
Carbohydrates	2 g
Cholesterol	5 mg
Sodium	98 mg

Honey-Mustard Dressing

Makes 3 servings

Good on greens as well as when served as a dip for fresh vegetables.

2 tablespoons (30 ml) honey
1 tablespoon (15 ml) Dijon mustard
1 tablespoon (15 ml) cider vinegar
1 tablespoon (15 ml) extra-virgin olive oil
1 tablespoon (15 ml) water
½ teaspoon (3 ml) lemon juice

Nutrition Per Serving	
Calories	87
Fat	5 g
Protein	0 g
Carbohydrates	12 g
Cholesterol	0 mg
Sodium	64 mg

Combine all the the ingredients and mix well. (If the honey is too thick to mix easily, you can heat it in the microwave for 5–10 seconds.)

★ Orange Vinaigrette

Makes 5 servings

An upscale version of your basic vinaigrette.

1 clove garlic, minced
1½ tablespoons (23 ml) chopped fresh parsley
1 teaspoon (5 ml) sugar
½ teaspoon (3 ml) salt
⅓ cup (80 ml) orange juice
2 tablespoons (30 ml) extra-virgin olive oil

Nutrition Per Serving	
Calories	63
Fat	5 g
Protein	0 g
Carbohydrates	4 g
Cholesterol	0 mg
Sodium	219 mg

In a small bowl, combine the garlic and parsley. Add the vinegar, sugar, and salt; mix well. Gradually add the orange juice and oil, stirring constantly. Blend well.

Chapter 11

Breads, Biscuits & Muffins

Everybody loves biting into a warm slice of bread fresh from the oven. However, when brainstorming on what type of recipes to include in this book, we originally left out breads. Why? Because of the time commitment involved. Well, after a little more research we discovered that breads can be as simple and quick to make as anything else. We've found some recipes that take very little time to prepare — no long hours of kneading — and leave the hard and lengthy work to the oven. Once the aroma begins to percolate through your apartment and out the door, you may find friends suddenly appearing on your doorstep. So enjoy your bread in good company.

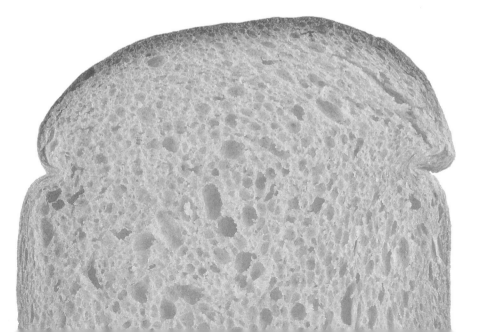

★Spice Loaf

Makes 10 servings

Spice Loaf is great any time: for breakfast, a snack, or dessert. While it is convenient to have an electric mixer when making this recipe, it's not essential.

1½ cups (375 ml) flour	½ teaspoon (3 ml) nutmeg
1½ teaspoons (8 ml) baking powder	5 tablespoons (75 ml) butter, chopped
½ teaspoon (3 ml) salt	2 egg whites
½ cup (125 ml) sugar	⅔ cup (160 ml) skim milk
1 teaspoon (5 ml) cinnamon	

1. Preheat the oven to 350°F (180°C).

2. In a large mixing bowl, combine the flour, baking powder, salt, sugar, cinnamon, and nutmeg. Mix well. Add the butter and mix thoroughly. Stir in the egg whites and milk.

3. Pour the batter into a greased 9 by 5-inch loaf pan. Place the pan on a cookie sheet in the center of the oven. Bake for 45 minutes, or until the top is golden brown. Cool the loaf on a rack before removing it from the pan.

Nutrition Per Serving

Calories	168
Fat	6 g
Protein	3 g
Carbohydrates	26 g
Cholesterol	16 mg
Sodium	239 mg

Mom's Tips

Keeping Milk On Hand

Keep a bag of powdered skim milk in your cupboard to use in making breads. This will save you money in the long run, especially if you're not a milk-drinker, since you won't have to buy carton upon carton of fresh milk for every recipe you try. When used in breads and muffins, rehydrated powdered skim milk tastes the same as the fresh stuff.

Whole Wheat Honey Biscuits

Makes 12 biscuits

Nutrition Per Serving

Calories	100
Fat	Less than 1 g
Protein	4 g
Carbohydrates	21 g
Cholesterol	0 mg
Sodium	2 mg

These biscuits are great to save for a quick breakfast with jam. The mixing and the baking won't take long, but you do have to wait for the dough to rise (30–40 minutes), so save this recipe for a day when you'll be at home studying.

1 cup (250 ml) lukewarm water
2 tablespoons (30 ml) active dry yeast
5 teaspoons (25 ml) honey
2½ cups (625 ml) whole wheat flour
Cooking spray

1. Pour the water into a large mixing bowl. Stir in the yeast and let sit until the mixture is slightly bubbly, about 10 minutes. Then add the honey and flour, and mix well.
2. Lightly coat a muffin tin (with at least 12 cups) with cooking spray. Fill each cup halfway with batter.
3. Let the muffin tin sit somewhere warm (next to a warm radiator, on top of a running dryer, or next to a preheating oven) until the batter has doubled in size (30–40 minutes).
4. While the dough is rising, preheat the oven to 350°F (180°C).
5. Bake for 20 minutes. Let sit in the tins for 5–10 minutes before removing.

Blueberry Scones

Makes 6 scones

For a different taste, substitute an equal amount of other berries or fruits for the blueberries.

- 1 cup (250 ml) all-purpose flour
- 3 tablespoons (45 ml) sugar
- 1½ teaspoons (8 ml) baking powder
- ½ teaspoon (3 ml) salt
- 1 teaspoon (5 ml) grated lemon rind
- 2 tablespoons (30 ml) margarine
- 1 egg
- 3 tablespoons (45 ml) skim milk
- ½ cup (125 ml) blueberries, washed and dried

1. Preheat the oven to 400°F (205°C).
2. In a mixing bowl, combine the flour, sugar, baking powder, salt, and lemon rind. Add the margarine and blend with a fork until mixture looks like rough crumbs.
3. In a separate bowl, combine the egg and milk. Add to the dry ingredients and mix thoroughly. Gently fold in the blueberries and stir well, until the dough comes cleanly off the sides of the bowl.
4. On a floured surface, knead the dough until it sticks together well. Add more flour if it's too sticky and clings to your hands.
5. Form the dough into six balls. Place them on a greased cookie sheet, and flatten each to about ¹/₂-inch thickness.
6. Bake for 12 minutes, until light brown on top. Allow to cool before eating.

Nutrition Per Serving	
Calories	155
Fat	5 g
Protein	3 g
Carbohydrates	25 g
Cholesterol	30 mg
Sodium	327 mg

Mom's Tips

Adding Fiber

Include extra fiber in your breads, muffins, and cookies by adding a touch of wheat bran or oat bran, some nuts, or fruit like raisins, apricots, or dates.

★ Zucchini Bread

Makes 12 servings

Our version is made with some healthy substitutes.

Nutrition Per Serving

Calories	208
Fat	7 g
Protein	3 g
Carbohydrates	33 g
Cholesterol	31 mg
Sodium	151 mg

1½ cups (375 ml) grated zucchini
1 cup (250 ml) all-purpose flour
½ cup (125 ml) oats
1½ teaspoons (8 ml) baking powder
2 teaspoons (10 ml) cinnamon
½ teaspoon (3 ml) salt
1 cup (250 ml) packed
  brown sugar
¼ teaspoon (1 ml) grated
  ginger (optional)
2 teaspoons (10 ml) vanilla
⅓ cup (80 ml) vegetable oil
⅓ cup (80 ml) applesauce
  (see page 119 for our recipe)
2 eggs, beaten

1. Preheat the oven to 350°F (180°C).
2. In a large mixing bowl, combine all the ingredients. Mix well.
3. Pour batter into a greased loaf pan and bake for 45 minutes, or until a knife inserted into the center comes out dry. Cool the loaf on a rack before removing it from the pan.

Pumpkin Bread

Makes 10 servings

You can find canned pumpkin pie filling at most grocery stores.

Nutrition Per Serving

Calories	213
Fat	7 g
Protein	3 g
Carbohydrates	36 g
Cholesterol	36 mg
Sodium	280 mg

2 eggs, beaten
1 cup (250 ml) sugar
¼ cup (125 ml) vegetable oil
¼ cup (125 ml) applesauce
  (see page 119 for our recipe)
1 10-ounce (285 g) can pumpkin pie filling
1½ cups (375 ml) all-purpose
  flour
1 teaspoon (5 ml) baking
  powder
1 teaspoon (5 ml) baking soda
1½ teaspoons (8 ml) cinnamon
½ teaspoon (3 ml) salt

1. Preheat the oven to 375°F (190°C).
2. In a bowl, combine the eggs and sugar. Mix in the oil and applesauce. Add the pumpkin filling and mix thoroughly.
3. In a separate bowl, combine the dry ingredients. Add to the wet ingredients and mix thoroughly.
4. Pour into a greased loaf pan. Bake for 1 hour.

 Beer Bread

Makes 8 servings

This is a speedy bread recipe that is best served with jam or honey. You can use any type of beer you prefer, including nonalcoholic.

3 cups (750 ml) all-purpose flour
3 tablespoons (45 ml) sugar
4 tablespoons (60 ml) active dry active yeast

1 12-ounce (342 g) bottle of beer
Nonstick cooking spray

Nutrition Per Serving	
Calories	224
Fat	Less than 1 g
Protein	7 g
Carbohydrates	44 g
Cholesterol	0 mg
Sodium	6 mg

1. In a large bowl, combine the flour, sugar, and yeast. Add the beer and mix well.

2. Spray the loaf pan with cooking spray; pour in the batter. Place in a cold oven and set to 350°F (180°C). Bake for 40–45 minutes, until a knife inserted in the center comes out clean. Cool the loaf on a rack before removing it from the pan.

Southwestern Corn Bread

Makes 6 servings

Corn bread is a delicious accompaniment to southwestern dishes, soups, and salads.

1 package corn bread/muffin mix
1 7-ounce (198 g) can creamed corn

1 tablespoon (15 ml) chopped jalepeño pepper
Honey for topping

Nutrition Per Serving	
Calories	124
Fat	2 g
Protein	2 g
Carbohydrates	25 g
Cholesterol	0 mg
Sodium	54 mg

1. Preheat the oven to 375°F (190°C).

2. Prepare the corn bread batter according to the package instructions. Stir in the creamed corn and chopped jalepeño.

3. Pour the batter into a greased loaf pan. Bake for 20 minutes, or until the top of the loaf springs back when touched in the center.

4. Spread honey over the top immediately upon removal from the oven. Let stand for five minutes before serving.

★Bran Muffins

Makes 12 muffins

These muffins make a great breakfast.

1 cup (250 ml) all-purpose flour
1 teaspoon (5 ml) baking powder
2 teaspoons (10 ml) baking soda
¼ teaspoon (1 ml) salt
⅔ cup (160 ml) sugar
½ teaspoon (3 ml) cinnamon

¾ cup (185 ml) bran cereal (flakes)
1 egg
½ cup (125 ml) skim milk
⅓ cup (80 ml) applesauce (see page 119 for our recipe)
½ cup (125 ml) orange juice

1. Preheat the oven to 350°F (180°C).
2. In a large bowl, combine the flour, baking powder, baking soda, salt, sugar, cinnamon, and bran cereal (don't crush the flakes).
3. In a separate bowl, beat the egg. Add the milk and applesauce, and mix until smooth. Combine the egg mixture with the dry ingredients and add the orange juice. Mix gently.
4. Fill greased muffin cups about ¾ full with the batter. Bake for about 15 minutes, until a knife inserted in the center comes out clean.

★Blueberry Muffins with Oats

Makes 15 muffins

Oats and applesauce help make a healthier version of this classic muffin recipe.

1½ cups (375 ml) flour
1 cup (250 ml) rolled oats
½ cup (125 ml) sugar
2 teaspoons (10 ml) baking powder
½ teaspoon (3 ml) salt
½ teaspoon (3 ml) nutmeg
1 cup (250 ml) skim milk

1 egg
1 teaspoon (5 ml) vanilla
3 tablespoons (45 ml) applesauce (see page 119 for our recipe)
1½ cups (375 ml) blueberries, rinsed and dried

Nutrition Per Serving	
Calories	108
Fat	1 g
Protein	4 g
Carbohydrates	20 g
Cholesterol	12 mg
Sodium	181 mg

1. Preheat the oven to 350°F (180°C).
2. In a large bowl, combine the flour, oats, sugar, baking powder, salt, and nutmeg.
3. In a separate bowl, mix the milk, egg, vanilla, and applesauce.
4. Combine the wet ingredients with the dry ingredients and mix thoroughly. Gently fold in the blueberries.
5. Fill greased muffin cups about ³/₄ full with the batter. Bake for 15–20 minutes, until a knife inserted in the center comes out clean.

Chapter 12

Dessert Time

We had trouble keeping this section short. Always an anticipated course during a meal, dessert lies close to practically everyone's heart. We've tried, as best we could, to provide you with a few recipes that should make our favorite part of the meal just a little healthier — but for all those who crave the traditional moist, rich flavor of a delicious chocolate cake fresh from the oven, we've included one of those as well.

Some hints in this section and throughout the book should provide you with options for making a recipe healthier while at the same time maintaining the recipe's texture and flavor. Don't go overboard, though — this is still dessert, and it wouldn't be dessert if it didn't include the temptation for just one more bite, offset by the growing pressure of your belt buckle. Have fun here, and when done, sit back and relax. If you've made it through cooking an entire meal on your own, then smile, feel accomplished, and pick up your fork for another bite of dessert.

Carrot Cake

Makes 12 servings

A moist and delicious cake. Great for entertaining.

Nutrition Per Serving	
Calories	197
Fat	7 g
Protein	3 g
Carbohydrates	32 g
Cholesterol	30 mg
Sodium	218 mg

1⅓ cups (330 ml) all-purpose flour
1 cup (250 ml) sugar
1½ teaspoons (8 ml) baking soda
1 teaspoon (5 ml) baking powder
1½ teaspoons (8 ml) cinnamon
½ teaspoon (3 ml) nutmeg
Pinch of salt
⅓ cup (80 ml) vegetable or canola oil
⅓ cup (80 ml) applesauce (see page 119 for our recipe)
2 eggs, beaten
1½ cups (375 ml) grated carrots

1. Preheat the oven to 350°F (180°C).
2. In a large mixing bowl, stir together the flour, sugar, baking soda, baking powder, cinnamon, and nutmeg. Sprinkle with salt.
3. Add the oil, applesauce, and eggs. Stir well. Add the carrots and mix.
4. Pour the batter into a greased and floured loaf pan and bake for about 30 minutes, or until a knife inserted into the cake's center comes out dry. Cool on a rack before removing from the pan.

Tropical Fruit Salad

Makes 4 servings

Sweet but light, this makes a great snack as well as a dessert.

Nutrition Per Serving	
Calories	86
Fat	Less than 1 g
Protein	1 g
Carbohydrates	22 g
Cholesterol	0 mg
Sodium	3 mg

1 mango, sliced
2 bananas, sliced
2 kiwi, sliced
3 tablespoons (45 ml) orange juice
1 tablespoon (15 ml) lemon juice

Mix the mango, banana, and kiwi. Stir in the orange and lemon juice.

Peaches and Cream

Makes 4 servings

A quick fix for a sugar craving.

Nutrition Per Serving	
Calories	129
Fat	5 g
Protein	1 g
Carbohydrates	24 g
Cholesterol	17 mg
Sodium	11 mg

4 whole peaches, peeled and chopped
1 lemon

½ cup (125 ml) low-fat whipped cream
¼ cup (60 ml) packed brown sugar

1. Preheat the broiler. Arrange the chopped peaches in a baking dish, spreading them out evenly, and squeeze lemon juice over them.
2. Cover evenly with whipped cream, then sprinkle with brown sugar.
3. Broil for 4 minutes, or until the top begins to turn golden.

Apple Cobbler

Makes 6 servings

This easy dessert can also be made with pears, peaches, or any other fruit that you desire.

Nutrition Per Serving	
Calories	121
Fat	3 g
Protein	2 g
Carbohydrates	23 g
Cholesterol	5 mg
Sodium	78 mg

4 large apples (Macintosh are best), peeled and thinly sliced
4 tablespoons (60 ml) flour
3 tablespoons (45 ml) apple juice
1 teaspoon (5 ml) cinnamon
A pinch of nutmeg

1 tablespoon (15 ml) butter, melted
1 tablespoon (15 ml) water
7 tablespoons (105 ml) graham cracker crumbs

1. Preheat the oven to 375°F (190°C).
2. In an 8 by 5-inch pan, toss together the apples, 2 tablespoons flour, and the apple juice, until the apple slices are well coated.
3. In a separate bowl, combine the remaining 2 tablespoons flour, the cinnamon, nutmeg, and graham cracker crumbs. Stir in the butter and water. Mix until pea-size clumps form.
4. Spread the graham cracker topping over the apples. Bake for 30 minutes, or until the topping is lightly browned.

Strawberry Shortcake

Makes 10 servings

This recipe makes about ten biscuits. If you're not planning on eating ten strawberry shortcakes, you may want to halve the ingredients for the strawberry topping. You can always go ahead and make the full ten biscuits—they're great plain or with jam.

Nutrition Per Serving	
Calories	141
Fat	5 g
Protein	2 g
Carbohydrates	22 g
Cholesterol	15 mg
Sodium	51 mg

½ cup (125 ml) skim milk
1 tablespoon (15 ml) lemon juice
1¼ cups (185 ml) flour
6 tablespoons (90 ml) sugar
⅓ teaspoon (3 ml) baking powder

2 tablespoons (30 ml) butter, softened
2 cups (500 ml) sliced strawberries
Light whipped cream to taste (approximately 1 tablespoon per person)

1. Preheat the oven to 475°F (250°C).
2. In a small bowl, stir together the milk and lemon juice.
3. In a separate bowl, mix the flour, sugar, and baking powder. Add the butter and cream until the mixture is of an even consistency. Add the lemon and milk and mix thoroughly.
4. Drop the batter in spoonfuls onto an ungreased baking sheet. Bake for about 15 minutes, or until the biscuits are golden brown.
5. Serve the biscuits covered with strawberries and topped with whipped cream.

★Banana Chocolate Chip Muffins

Makes 12 muffins

This is one of our favorite dessert recipes.

½ cup (125 ml) vegetable shortening
1 cup (250 ml) sugar
2 cups (500 ml) all-purpose flour
2 eggs
½ teaspoon (3 ml) salt

3 large (or 5 small) very ripe bananas
1 teaspoon (5 ml) baking soda
1 teaspoon (5 ml) baking powder
⅔ cup (160 ml) mini chocolate chips

1. Preheat the oven to 350°F (180°C).
2. In a mixing bowl, cream together the shortening and sugar. Add 1 tablespoon flour to the mixture. Beat in eggs one at a time.
3. In a separate bowl, mash the bananas to a soft pulp.
4. Set aside ¹/₂ cup flour. Add the remaining flour and the banana pulp to the creamed mixture, mixing it in bit by bit.
5. In a separate bowl, stir the reserved ¹/₂ cup flour with the salt, baking soda, and baking powder. Add the chocolate chips, tossing to coat.
6. Stir together the dry and creamed mixtures. Pour the batter into well-greased muffin tins and bake for 25 minutes, or until a knife inserted in the center of a muffin comes out clean.

Blueberry Coffee Cake

Makes 6 servings

Good for both dessert and breakfast.

2 tablespoons (30 ml) butter
¾ cup (185 ml) sugar
2 eggs (one separated)
1¼ cup (310 ml) plus 1 tablespoon (15 ml) water
¼ teaspoon (1 ml) salt
¾ cup (185 ml) flour
1 teaspoon (5 ml) baking powder
1 egg yolk
1½ cups (375 ml) blueberries, rinsed

Nutrition Per Serving	
Calories	238
Fat	6 g
Protein	4 g
Carbohydrates	42 g
Cholesterol	106 mg
Sodium	211 mg

1. Preheat the oven to 300°F (150°C).
2. In a small bowl, cream together the butter and ¼ cup sugar.
3. In a large bowl, beat one egg, then add the water. Stir in the salt, flour, and baking powder, then mix in the butter and sugar mixture.
4. Spread the batter in a greased pie pan. Top with blueberries.
5. In a small bowl, mix the egg yolk and remaining ½ cup sugar. Sprinkle over the blueberries
6. Bake for 35 minutes.

Gingerbread

Makes 12 servings

A favorite when topped with whipped cream or ice cream.

1½ cups (375 ml) all-purpose flour
1½ teaspoons (8 ml) baking soda
1 teaspoon (5 ml) grated fresh ginger
1½ teaspoons (8 ml) cinnamon
1 egg beaten
¼ cup (60 ml) sugar
⅓ cup (80 ml) molasses
½ cup (125 ml) boiling water
¼ cup (60 ml) vegetable oil
¼ cup (60 ml) applesauce (see page 119 for our recipe)

Nutrition Per Serving	
Calories	148
Fat	5 g
Protein	2 g
Carbohydrates	24 g
Cholesterol	15 mg
Sodium	54 mg

1. Preheat the oven to 350°F (180°C).
2. In a large bowl, combine the flour, baking soda, ginger, and cinnamon, and mix well. Stir in the egg, sugar, and molasses. Add the water, oil, and applesauce, and mix until the batter is smooth.
3. Pour the batter into a greased square baking pan and bake for 30 minutes.

Lemon Almond Biscotti

Makes 15 bars

These Italian treats, great with coffee, are actually quite simple to make at home.

- **1** cup (250 ml) all-purpose flour
- **⅓** cup (80 ml) sugar
- **⅓** cup (80 ml) whole unblanched almonds
- **1** tablespoon (15 ml) grated lemon rind
- **½** tablespoon (8 ml) baking powder
- **1** tablespoon (45 ml) vegetable olive oil
- **1** egg whites
- **½** teaspoon (3 ml) vanilla

1. Preheat the oven to 325°F (165°C).
2. In a large bowl, combine the flour, sugar, almonds, lemon rind, and baking powder.
3. In a separate bowl, mix the oil, egg, and vanilla. Combine the wet and dry ingredients and stir well. The batter should be sticky.
4. Roll the dough into a log about 1 foot long and place on a greased and floured cookie sheet. Bake for 35 minutes.
5. Remove from the oven, and allow to cool for 5 minutes. Cut the biscotti into 3/4-inch slices and lay the pieces on their sides on the baking sheet.
6. Bake for 10 minutes more. Cool.

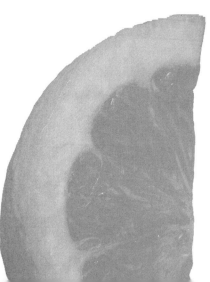
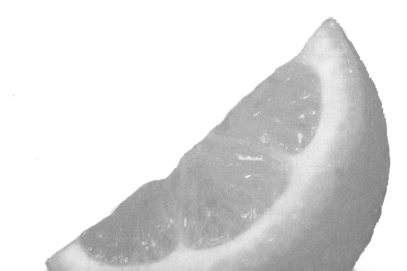

★ Peanut Butter Cookies

Makes 30 cookies

For more variety, try adding peanut butter chips or chocolate chips.

4 tablespoons (60 ml)
  unsalted butter, softened
¾ cup (185 ml) packed
  brown sugar
¾ cup (185 ml) peanut butter
1 egg

¼ cup (60 ml) applesauce
  (see page 119 for our recipe)
1 teaspoon (5 ml) vanilla extract
1½ cups (375 ml) flour
¾ teaspoon (4 ml) baking soda

Nutrition Per Serving	
Calories	99
Fat	5 g
Protein	2 g
Carbohydrates	12 g
Cholesterol	10 mg
Sodium	67 mg

1. Preheat the oven to 375°F (190°C).
2. In a mixing bowl, combine the butter, brown sugar, and peanut butter and blend well. Stir in the applesauce, vanilla, and egg.
3. In a separate bowl, combine the flour and baking soda. Gradually add the dry ingredients to the wet ingredients. Mix thoroughly.
4. Drop spoonfuls of dough onto an ungreased cookie sheet. Gently press each piece of dough with a fork. (Press twice to make a criss-cross pattern.) Bake for 8 minutes.

Apple Custard

Makes 4 servings

This recipe is particularly good with Macintosh apples.

1 tablespoon (15 ml) butter
3 cups (750 ml) peeled and
  sliced apples
¼ cup (60 ml) skim milk
3 tablespoons (45 ml)
  all-purpose flour

1½ tablespoons (23 ml) sugar
1 egg
1⅓ tablespoons (23 ml)
  baking powder
1 teaspoon (5 ml) cinnamon

Nutrition Per Serving	
Calories	133
Fat	4 g
Protein	3 g
Carbohydrates	23 g
Cholesterol	53 mg
Sodium	459 mg

1. Preheat the oven to 350°F (180°C).
2. In a skillet over medium heat, melt the butter. Add the apples and sauté until tender.
3. In a mixing bowl, blend together all other ingredients until smooth.
4. Spread the apples in a shallow baking dish, forming a level layer. Pour in the batter, covering the apples completely. Bake for 40 minutes, or until a knife inserted in the center comes out clean.

Oatmeal Chocolate Chip Cookies

Makes 24 cookies

A classic cookie recipe. Also good with raisins.

½ cup (250 ml) unsalted butter, softened
¼ cup (60 ml) applesauce (see page 119 for our recipe)
½ cup (125 ml) packed brown sugar
½ cup (125 ml) granulated sugar
1 egg

2 teaspoons (10 ml) vanilla
2 cups (500 ml) flour
½ teaspoon (3 ml) cinnamon
½ teaspoon (3 ml) salt
½ teaspoon (3 ml) baking soda
1½ cups (375 ml) uncooked "quick" oatmeal
1 cup (250 ml) chocolate chips

1. Preheat the oven to 350°F (180°C).
2. In a bowl, combine the butter, applesauce, brown sugar, granulated sugar, egg, and vanilla. Mix thoroughly.
3. In a separate bowl, combine the flour, cinnamon, salt, and baking soda. Gradually mix the dry ingredients into the wet ingredients; add the oatmeal and chocolate chips. Stir well.
4. Drop spoonfuls of dough onto a greased cookie sheet. Bake for 10–15 minutes. Let cool before removing from the cookie sheet.

Mom's Chocolate Cake

Makes 15 servings

You got us on this one — it's not the least bit healthy. But it does lift the spirits. The secret ingredient is the coffee.

Nutrition Per Serving	
Calories	246
Fat	9 g
Protein	4 g
Carbohydrates	41 g
Cholesterol	25 mg
Sodium	280 mg

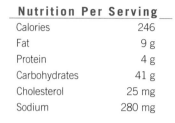

- 1¾ cups (435 ml) flour
- 2 cups (500 ml) sugar
- ¾ cup (185 ml) cocoa
- 2 teaspoons (10 ml) baking soda
- 1 teaspoon (5 ml) baking powder
- ½ teaspoon (3 ml) salt
- 2 eggs
- 1 cup (250 ml) strong black coffee
- 1 cup (250 ml) skim milk
- 2 tablespoons (30 ml) lemon juice
- ½ cup (125 ml) vegetable oil
- 1 teaspoon (5 ml) vanilla

1. Preheat the oven to 350°F (180°C).
2. In a bowl, combine the flour, sugar, cocoa, baking soda, baking powder, and salt.
3. In a separate bowl, combine the eggs, coffee, milk, lemon juice, oil, and vanilla. Add the dry ingredients and stir. The mixture will look lumpy.
4. Pour into a greased 13 by 9-inch cake pan. Bake for about 45 minutes, until a knife inserted in the center comes out clean.

Index

Other Storey Titles You Will Enjoy

101 Perfect Chocolate Chip Cookies, by Gwen Steege. Whether you like your chocolate chip cookies with or without nuts, chewy or crumbly, traditional, exotic, healthy, adventurous, decadent, or completely over-the-top, you'll find the perfect recipe here. 144 pages. Paperback. ISBN 1-58017-312-8

The College Cookbook, by Geri Harrington. From more than 55 college and universities across North America, here are 200 original recipes designed for the busy and (often) broke college student. Updated edition. 160 pages. Paperback. ISBN 0-88266-497-2.

Dorm Room Feng Shui, by Katherine Olaksen with Elizabeth MacCrellish and Margaret M. Donahue. Every college student faces the same quandaries—getting along with a sloppy roommate, coping with a disappointing grade, the forever-empty wallet—but who would have ever thought that the solution to these and many other campus woes could be in the arrangement of dorm rooms? Here, Olaksen shares her very real and practical feng shui solutions to these and other typical collegiate problems. 144 pages. Paperback. ISBN 1-58017-592-9.

Every Woman's Quick & Easy Car Care, by Bridget Kachur. This user-friendly guide is your complete Auto Mechanics 101. Any woman with an open mind and a willing hand can follow these simple, step-by-step tutorials. 288 pages. Flexibind. ISBN 1-58017-451-5.

Healing Tonics, by Jeanine Pollak. Bring the juice bar home with these simple, nourishing recipes for drinks that can help boost mental clarity, increase stamina, aid digestion, support heart health, and more. 160 pages. Paperback. ISBN 1-58017-240-7.

Mom's Best Desserts: 100 Classic Treats that taste as Good Now as They Did Then, Andrea Chesman and Fran Raboff. Here are the recipes that everyone remembers from mom's kitchen, presented in easy-to-follow recipes for today's bakers. 224 pages. Paperback. ISBN 1-58017-480-9.

Munchies, by Kevin Telles Roberts. 110 delicious, totally accessible recipes that are quick to prepare, satisfying to eat, and impressive to serve to friends. 192 pages. Paperback. ISBN 1-58017-536-8.

The One-Minute Organizer Plain & Simple, by Donna Smallin. These 500 simple and painless quick fixes offer solutions to the busy person's daily battle with clutter, both physical and mental, one minute at a time. 256 pages. Paperback. ISBN 1-58017-584-4.

These and other books from Storey Publishing are available wherever quality books are sold or by calling 1-800-441-5700. Visit us at www.storey.com.

Today is your lucky day